Rebekah

The Voice of God

Brenda Adams

Published by: King's Way Publishing
A division of King's Way Enterprises, Inc.
27 Dawson Drive, Fredericksburg, VA. 22405

ISBN: 1502561107

ISBN 13: 9781502561107

LCCN: 2014921551

Dedication

I'd like to dedicate this book to the ones who took this journey with me; without their love and support, I would not have made it through. My wonderful husband Frank's faithful love and support guided and comforted me through the long and dark nights. My precious daughter Miranda paid a great price and yet has become a beautiful young woman and remains the joy of my life.

My mother Merilyn's prayers, wisdom, and courage, and her many hours holding onto Rebekah in the rocking chair helped to bring her baby granddaughter into the presence of God. And my dad, Troy Parkman, was always there for us helping, rocking Becky, and soothing her with his "It'll Be All Right in the Middle of the Night" song.

Most of all I dedicate this book and its message to the Good Shepherd, Jesus Christ. Thank You for coming after me.

Contents

Introduction

The Bible teaches us that Jesus, the Good Shepherd, leaves the ninety-nine who are safe in the fold and goes after the one who has strayed. Finding that one, Jesus ministers what the stray needs and carries the stray safely back to the fold on His shoulders. What a wonderful picture of the love of God.

This is a story about the love and mercy of God at work in the lives of one family to manifest His glory and goodness.

I didn't realize that I was drifting from safety; I didn't realize that I was ignoring God's voice. I didn't realize that I was living my life separate from Him. He had been trying for years to get my attention, yet I continued to go my own way, doing everything in my own strength and according to my way of thinking. Although I loved the Lord, I had not given much thought to the subject of Christ's lordship.

God is always speaking, but we don't always want to hear what He is saying. He whispers, and He calls; He nudges, and He gives us signs along the way. Sometimes we pay attention, and sometimes we don't. He is long-suffering and patient. But there comes a time when, after we have turned a deaf ear and continue to step over the barriers that He puts in our way, He must speak loudly because He is so loving and kind.

In 1985, God spoke loudly to me. His voice came to me at 10:05 a.m. on Friday, July 19, in the form of a beautiful little girl with blue eyes and ash-blond hair to whom, I am sure, only the angels in heaven have anything that can compare.

She did not come to ride a bicycle or to play with dolls, but instead to be the voice of God that would captivate her mother's heart, to set me free from my self-sufficiency and independent living, and to return me safely to the fold.

Her name was Rebekah, and she was the voice of God to me.

Dear brothers and sisters, when trouble comes your way, consider it an opportunity for great joy (James 1:2 NLT [New Living Translation]).

Preface

Frank and I married in 1968. We received the call into full-time ministry two years later and began a journey that would not only teach us how to love each other, but would also equip us to walk with God.

I had received Christ as my Savior at the age of ten and by seventeen had made an all-out commitment of my life to Christ. I had been blessed with a Christian heritage that lay a good foundation early in life.

Frank, on the other hand, had only been in church a few times in his life when I met him in 1967. No one in his family was a Christian at the time, and he had lived a very worldly lifestyle.

I found myself engaged to a man who was not a Christian, had no intention of building a life with God as the head, and could barely function in life.

One month before our intended wedding date, Frank went AWOL from the military. He was arrested for drunk and disorderly conduct and landed in the Winter Haven, Florida, city jail. While there Frank found Jesus. We were married two months later, and I have since watched as Jesus fulfilled His promise to me from Joel 2:25 (NLT): "I will restore the years that the moth and the canker worm has eaten away." To this day I have never seen a man more intent on becoming whole. Frank realized the magnitude of his brokenness and knew in his heart that the answers would be found in the Word of God. Over the forty-five years that we have been married, I have watched Frank give himself to God and His Word. I have watched as God faithfully transformed his life and used Frank mightily in His service. Frank is a very gifted and compassionate anointed minister.

During our Bible school years, I became pregnant. While visiting friends, I became very sick and was taken to a country doctor who made a very wise diagnosis that I had an ectopic pregnancy. Frank was instructed to get me quickly to my own doctor for surgery.

My doctor dispelled the diagnosis and concluded that I was having a normal menstrual period. I would continue to bleed for the next four weeks. My body began to swell, the pain increased and there were times when I would faint.

On one occasion I had to be taken to the ER and kept overnight. While there the tube ruptured, but this wasn't realized until later when it was discussed with the doctor in Florida who eventually performed the surgery. I was discharged with the diagnosis of being anemic, but no one discovered the ruptured tube.

At some point in the four weeks my appendix ruptured. I lived for a month with a ruptured ectopic pregnancy, a ruptured appendix and internal hemorraging. All the while I continued to go to my regular doctor who said that it was all in my head and I should just "ride it out."

Upon the arrival of my parents I agreed to go home to Florida with them to see a doctor. After my examination with the new doctor Mom and I were told that I had half enough blood in my body to be alive and that he had outlined the mass in my stomach. I would have to have emergency surgery and that he did not see how that I could live.

It was my twenty-first birthday. While in emergency surgery, my temperature rose to 104 degrees and doctors found four stages of hemorrhaging. For days my family was told that there was no way that I could stay alive.

But God had a different plan.

After my recovery, I was told that I had lost my reproductive organs on the left side, and that the right side was so damaged that I would never become pregnant again. If by some miracle I did conceive, there was absolutely no way that I could carry a child.

The years that followed proved this diagnosis to be true. We tried everything, but nothing could be done; it was impossible. Specialists determined that there was too much damage to the remaining Fallopian tube.

Over the next ten years, my heart grieved for a child. God was faithful, and in 1981 we adopted our precious Miranda Renee, who was the fulfillment of my heart's desire. She was all I ever needed. My life with her was perfect.

By this time we had been in ministry for about eight years and had served in a pastoral capacity. Frank was successfully running his own construction business, too.

In 1984 we began pastoring a small home-mission church on the outskirts of Orlando, Florida. It was very hard work, and we had been hurt, as happens all too often in church life. Up until this time, I had been very self-sufficient. I really didn't need God. If anything difficult happened, I fixed it myself, changed the circumstances, or ran. On the outside, you'd never know that I was captain of my own vessel. Jesus was my Savior, and I loved Him, but He was not the Lord of my life.

I had been a good pastor's wife. But I became very unhappy with my living conditions and began to deceive my husband about what I felt was the will of God. I finally convinced him to leave the little church. Upon leaving the church, I made a list of "I will nots": I will not pastor another church. Frank will not pastor again—our denomination does not allow divorced men to hold pastoral positions, and I will divorce him if he goes back into ministry. We began to be "good to ourselves." We planned to make money and determined that we would never be hurt again. We went back into business. We headed toward a worldly lifestyle.

But God stood in our way.

One month after we left the little church, I

conceived Rebekah, whose name, oddly enough, means "a noose" or "to tie up."

Over the next four years, the voice of God heard through this little girl of miraculous conception changed our lives forever.

The will of God will always take you where you are incapable of doing what you need to do. Only His intervention and power can give you strength to accomplish what needs to be done.

Chapter 1

She Comes

You made all the delicate, inner parts of my body and knit me together in my mother's womb. Thank You for making me so wonderfully complex! Your workmanship is marvelous, how well I know it. You watched me as I was being formed in utter seclusion, as I was woven together in the dark of the womb. You saw me before I was born. Every day of my life was recorded in Your book. Every moment was laid out before a single day had passed. How precious are Your thoughts about me O God (Psalm 139:13–17 NLT).

At each examination throughout my pregnancy, my doctor would say, "Strong heartbeat; the baby has a very strong heart." This statement served to assure me that all was well. Being pregnant at the age of thirty-five, I was considered a high risk. I was offered an amniocentesis, but I was also made aware of the risks involved. If a problem were discovered, termination of the pregnancy would be the solution. Since that "solution" was out of the question, I declined the test.

Much later we would realize that Rebekah's heart was beating so strongly to compensate for an underdeveloped heart.

My pregnancy went well with no problems, and I took very good care of myself. My contractions began at 1:00 a.m. on July 19, 1985. Frank, my mother, and I went to the hospital, fully expecting to deliver a perfect baby. Throughout nine hours of labor, I watched the hands of the wall clock circle each hour. Soon we would be introduced to our child, the miracle child, the one who was formed by God in my womb. Soon we would have our answers. Would it be a boy or a girl? Who would he or she look like? Would he or she have Frank's beautiful blue eyes, as I hoped?

Soon I would be able to hold in my arms the child that I had loved and nurtured in my belly—in that special place just beneath my heart. Soon I would be able to look into the beautiful eyes of heaven's creation and see our destiny in our miracle child. And Miranda would become the big sister that would enjoy having a playmate and new guest at our tea parties.

I watched the clock intently; I wanted to know the exact moment that our little one would enter our world. The numbers are forever captured in my memory—10:05 a.m.

When we knew that the birth was minutes away, my mother told me that she was going to step across the hall until after the birth, and then she would return. My doctor, his nurse, Frank, and I welcomed our darling Rebekah.

Mother told me later that five minutes before Rebekah was born, there was a holy hush that filled the room, and she heard babies cry. In scripture there are times when this silence precedes something significant that God is doing—something that is part of His perfect plan. We didn't know that heaven had released its "angel on assignment." We had no idea how this baby would change our lives.

> *His secret purpose framed from the beginning [is] to bring us to our full glory (1 Corinthians 2:7 NEB [New English Bible]).*

When I saw my precious baby girl, I had no idea that anything was wrong. When she was placed upon my chest, I didn't have a clue that she wasn't the perfect baby that we had expected. Frank and I were elated that our sweet girl was here, and we were rejoicing at heaven's gift. We didn't realize that her limp and outstretched arms were "a sign." We didn't realize that her cry had a tone different from that of "normal" babies. Many things were obvious indications to those around us that something was very wrong, but to us, Rebekah was the culmination of all our hopes and dreams. There was no doubt that she was a miracle—a miracle conception after thirteen years of barrenness. Surely, then, she was perfect, because miracles are perfect.

But the doctor determined that our little girl was born with Down syndrome, and she was considered different from other babies. "Mongoloid"—every time the doctor and nurses said the word, chills went down my spine. They said it with such a cold tone in their voices. I could tell that the doctor and nurses wanted to be compassionate, but they were textbook with their pronouncement of our child as a Mongoloid. They weren't even kind enough to use the phrase "Down syndrome." Down the hall there were girl babies, and there were boy babies, and then there was our baby—a Down baby.

We were handed literature with pictures of babies and older people with Down syndrome, who were portrayed in a very negative way. But what about our baby? There was something inside us that wouldn't allow us to label our baby a Mongoloid and seal her fate to the distortions in the pictures. That couldn't possibly be our little girl's future. The medical staff told us there was no hope for her, and they waited for our decision to follow their advice and place her into a facility that could adequately care for her. They claimed it was for her own good and that we would be able to live our lives free from this sadness and "encumbrance."

They remarked that we certainly didn't want to take this child home where our daughter would see her and have to experience the uncertainties of our future. They cautioned us to spare our other daughter this pain and shame. I heard those words, and I wondered what century we were living in and why the medical staff fell back on the options of years gone by. But the doctor and nurses were insistent in their recommendations.

The staff began to enter my room with expressions of sympathy and sorrow for our loss. The air in the room became heavy as our hearts were torn from our bodies. Even now as I write years later, I cannot completely put the depth of our sorrow and the intensity of our pain into words. It seemed as though at any moment my heart would burst from my body and explode in midair.

I felt that the earth had stopped, and I had walked up to its edge. How could this happen to our baby? I had done all the right things; we prayed, we believed, and yet our baby was born with Down syndrome. Where was God? If He had been here, this surely would not have happened.

I turned to Frank, desperately searching for an answer, for an open door, for a way out; surely he would have the answer to make it all right, to change the diagnosis. Surely it was all a mistake, and at any moment, someone would come bursting through the door to apologize for the terrible mistake that was made. But Frank's eyes met mine, and he said, "Honey, all I know is that the Bible says that the rain falls on the just and the unjust, and we just have to keep walking and see what God does." So that is what we decided to do—just keep on walking.

No apology came, and no mistake had been made; our baby was born with Down syndrome, or trisomy 21.

We waited for hours as more doctors were consulted on her condition. In my room the cold, still reality surrounded me like walls of doom that loomed higher than the ceiling. The room felt like a tomb of hopelessness, with no air, no light, and no seams in the walls that I could rip open and escape.

Somehow, along with the negative literature we received, a little book made its way into our hands that helped us to see that our darling Rebekah was not what the hospital staff said she was. Instead, she was truly a very special little girl come to help us discover the true treasures in life.

So we took our little Rebekah home – our sweet Becky; we got to know her, and we found that she was an earthly expression of God's love. The palmar crease in her hands, the fold at the back of her neck, and the space between her big toe and the next one were simply markings that made her Rebekah. After all, we all have markings on our bodies that help to make up our own uniqueness. These markings did not need to be labels; they just made her who she was. She was wonderfully formed in my womb by our heavenly Father, and He had a perfect plan for her life. Heaven had kissed the earth the morning she was born, and Rebekah was the result of the kiss.

When I looked into her face, I was awesomely aware of God's presence and purposes. I would get lost in her smile. Time would stop, and I would find myself realizing that nothing else mattered but this child: so much love, so much peace, and so much the reality of God's love. Her eyes seemed to peer into my very soul. The scripture speaks of "dove eyes" (Song of Solomon 1:15), and that is what she had: dove eyes. It was as though God had carved out part of His heart, placed it in this tiny little girl, and sent her on a mission. I didn't think that anyone could be around her for very long without being aware that there was something very heavenly about her.

One day, as I held her in my arms and gazed into her face, I said to my mom, "I wonder if Rebekah is an angel. But if she is, then when her job is done, she will leave us." I had no idea that my words would be a prophecy.

As we worked with her, we found that she was responsive. Her development of motor skills went well; at three months of age, she was performing the gross motor tasks of a four-month-old. All she would need was a little extra help to develop into a fully functioning individual.

Preparations for This Day

Early in my walk with the Lord, I had established what I call the four foundational stones of my life and relationship with Father God. These foundational stones have guided me through all of life and would serve as the saving grace that I needed in the darkest times of my life.

Our foundations determine the stature, strength, and value of the life we build. If our foundation is unsure, then all of life will be unsure, weak, and unstable, and we will never come to any maturity. Our growth will be stunted, and we will be crippled; we will fall victim to every negative circumstance that comes our way. If our foundation is misplaced by something or someone, then we will crumble under the slightest amount of pressure.

The tragedies in life challenge our understanding of God and His love. We ask, "How could a loving God not only allow, but also have purpose in such injustice?" We believe our question is justified, but our lack of understanding alone brings the character of God into question.

> *God is just in all His ways and kind in all His doings (Deuteronomy 32:4).*

He alone holds all the pieces of the puzzle. He knows the end from the beginning and is in control of everything in between. God is good, and He does good.

If I had put my trust in man, wealth, or the world's values, I would have ended up a statistic, like so many others do when tragedy comes into their lives. Our family would have been doomed to despair and destruction by life's unfair circumstances.

I am so grateful for the truth that God had placed deep within my heart, truth that was put to the ultimate test and proven. Our journey proved that God's Word is true— "We are more than conquerors through Christ" (Romans 8:37)—and He promises that when we go through fire it will not harm us. He did not say that we would be free of pain or struggle. But when we rely on His grace and go on through, the fire will not harm; it will bring good.

These foundation stones that are as essential as the air I breathe are 1) the justice of God, 2) God's sovereignty, 3) the righteousness of Christ, and 4) God's faithfulness. When we know and apply the truth of these attributes of God to our lives, we will be able to pilot safely to the other shore, no matter what storm may arise in the sea of life.

My understanding of the sovereignty of God brought on such confusion as I was given the news that Rebekah had Down syndrome. How could God? I knew that God was in control of every detail of life. There aren't some things He controls and others He leaves to the roll of the dice. I knew that God had not only sent my child, but He had created her with Down syndrome.

We never have complete understanding of the ways of God – "we know in part" 1Corinthians 13:9 – but when Christ comes in the fulfillment of all things, we will know in full. We continue to move and grow in the knowledge of God and His ways as we work through circumstances that we face and allow God to reveal Himself. Ever situation is an opportunity to grow in understanding. I knew about God's sovereignty, but it was limited by my experience. This experience would bring me to a much greater understanding.

You knew me…You formed me in my mother's womb (Psalm 139:13).

God formed her; put her spirit within her; and created her little, creased hands and neck fold. All of the identifying marks associated with Down syndrome were created by God.

I knew these things, but still they didn't line up with the idea of "the good and perfect gift" that I had associated with the goodness of God. I thought good things were supposed to be pretty and painless. The picture of our future was not pretty, and it certainly was not painless.

Suddenly, the future that we had planned had changed; everything was different. How? What? When? These questions flooded our minds. We were certainly in uncharted waters; we were strangers to special-needs children. Now our future would have to unfold daily—and sometimes moment by moment—as we struggled to find our way. The only unchanged things in our lives were the promises of God.

The unexpected and sometimes tragic issues in life are hard to embrace and reckon; how can things that we perceive as ugly and unwanted bring about goodness and blessings? How do we see goodness and beauty in people bound to wheelchairs, stitched and disfigured faces, crippled children, and all the world's other injustices?

Ann Voskamp wrote in *One Thousand Gifts*, "[This] is what the French call *d'un beau affreux,* what the Germans call *hubsch-hasslich*—the ugly-beautiful. That which is perceived as ugly transfigures into beautiful…The ugly can be beautiful. The dark can give birth to life; suffering can deliver grace."

Chapter 2

Something Is Wrong

And God is able to make all grace abound toward you, that you always having all sufficiency in all things, may have abundance for every good work (2 Corinthians 9:8).

For three short months, our little family enjoyed our sweet baby girl. We got to know her and found that she wasn't anything like we were told. She brought us all enormous joy. We gave her love, and she gave back so much more. Miranda tried to care for her like she did her baby dolls, and Rebekah adored her big sister. Whenever Miranda, who was four years old at the time, would enter the room, Rebekah would lock her eyes on her and follow her everywhere she went, taking in everything that Miranda did with total amazement. Miranda would wrap her sister up in her arms and sing to her in our rocking chair, while Rebekah soaked in every word and touch that were so uniquely Miranda's.

We were a family just like every other—well, almost. I dressed Rebekah in the same beautiful dresses that I had put on Miranda. I put the same lace socks on her feet and the same hairpieces in her hair that her big sister had worn. She was no different, but then she was very different. I would dress her up to go for an appointment or to go shopping and would be breathless at her beauty, only to find that the public did not share my assessment. How could they not see that she was heaven-sent and that she was beautiful? How could they not be aware of the almost holy presence that was hers?

People stared and whispered. It didn't seem to matter that I saw them staring and heard them whispering. All that seemed to matter to people was that she was different, and we all know what that means. You are excluded from the norm when you are different. All I wanted to do was to protect Rebekah from other people's stares. We knew she was perfect in all of the areas that mattered. Her spirit and her emotions were intact and perfect. She was God's creation.

We tried our best to live a normal life while feeling a mixture of emotions that included grief over the loss of the normal child that we expected and the joy of getting to know this beautiful creature that had been given to us. We had confidence that "all things work together for good to those called according to His purpose" (Romans 8:28), but we lived with the sick and sinking feeling of not knowing how to go on and build a life that was now so different from what we had expected. With every positive there was a conflicting negative—such a mixture—but we were convinced that God was in control and that somehow it would all be OK.

At three and a half months of age, Rebekah contracted an upper respiratory infection; she would get uncomfortable in the afternoons, and her temperature would rise. We took Rebekah to Miranda's regular pediatrician, who listened to her heart and immediately knew that there was a big problem.

Rebekah was placed in the care of a pediatric cardiologist, who discovered that she had a small hole in her heart, an endocardial cushion defect that would require surgery to place a small patch in the heart. We were told that Rebekah was too young for the surgery and that we should wait until she was closer to a year old.

Rebekah was treated with antibiotics for the respiratory infection, but she continued to spike a temperature during the afternoon. By this time everything was viewed as part of the cardiac problem, and no other avenues were even considered. Much later we would realize that she was allergic to the oral antibiotics. They caused her stomach pain and anxiety, which resulted in a rise in her temperature. But for the time being, she was hospitalized and placed on six weeks of IV antibiotics to combat the threat of infection moving into the heart. Even these antibiotics caused severe stomach pain, which resulted in intense screaming. At times, we felt as though we had lost her to the pain, and all we could do was watch.

All the while, those "dove eyes" begged for our intervention, for rescue from a world of torture that she didn't understand. Many times we wanted to grab her and run for the nearest door to a place of safety; but we knew what would happen to us if we tried any such thing.

We would eventually learn that the doctors never realized that the medication that they thought was helping her was the very source of the problem. They added a new drug that they hoped would ease Rebekah's pain. The hospital pharmacy did not stock the drug, and the nurses had never heard of it. It did seem to ease the pain at first, but after an hour or so, the pain began to return. I asked the nurse when Rebekah would receive more of the drug, since it seemed to help. But after Rebekah did receive a second dose, her extremities turned bright red, and she began to have a respiratory reaction. The cardiologist was not called as we requested, but a third-year resident examined her and determined that she was OK and that we were simply overreactive parents. The nurses on duty were very concerned, and they researched the drug. At our insistence the hospital finally called the cardiologist, who confirmed that Rebekah had indeed had a respiratory reaction to the new drug that was given. She was diagnosed as being in respiratory distress. But she finally calmed down, and we thought everything would be OK.

Mom and I would take turns spending the night to care for Rebekah. It was my mother's turn to stay the night, and I went home to get some rest. During the night

Rebekah's intense pain returned. Mother walked and rocked Rebekah, who was hooked to an IV line, all night. Rebekah was also given a "relaxer," chloral hydrate, five times during the night, and each dose slowed her respiration.

Frank and I got to the hospital early the next morning to find Rebekah in trouble. I took her into my arms and saw the helplessness in her eyes. The nurse came and shot yet another dose of chloral hydrate into her mouth.

Here was a baby already in respiratory distress, who had received five doses through the night, and then another dose in the morning. When I heard the liquid gurgling in the back of Rebekah's throat, I ran, with Rebekah in my arms, to catch the eye of a nurse whom we trusted. She ran, grabbed Rebekah, and turned her on her stomach. Rebekah was in respiratory arrest and was put on a respirator. She was placed in an ICU where, in my opinion, she was butchered and neglected before she was finally released to the hospital that would do her heart surgery. Rebekah left that ICU with seven staph infections.

I realized after many years that the medical staff at the ICU did not intentionally butcher or abuse my daughter, but nonetheless that was my perception at the time. On three occasions, we had to prevent overdoses of heart medication. Rebekah's chart read, "Mom gives meds," in large red letters, and yet nurses in training had to be stopped from administering a second dose of her heart medication, which would have had severe complications. We watched as unskilled lab technicians would rip and tear her delicate skin while trying to draw what seemed to be extraordinary amounts of blood. They shaved her head; they put IV lines in her head and neck but left them in too long, which resulted in backups that left large scars over her head and body. Many things happened that resulted in our slowly losing unique aspects of Rebekah, but the greatest loss was that of her beautiful smile. We loved to look into her face and smile and to see her beautiful smile break out to engulf us. Her smile would light the room when she was filled with joy. But now she had so little to smile about. And after the respiratory arrest we never saw her smile again. I thought that that would be too much to lose, but we did. We never saw that smile again.

In the ICU we saw babies, including our own, left screaming and unattended. When a baby on a respirator screams, no sound comes out. All we could see were their little mouths stretched open, and we knew that they were in pain. Staff in the room can walk about tending to their business while the babies scream; the babies can be ignored. On one occasion we came in to the ICU and found that the small, lightweight respirator hose that usually crossed Rebekah's face had been replaced with a large, black, heavy one that dripped water slowly onto her face. We were alarmed; to us it seemed like water torture. We immediately called a nurse's attention to the dripping water; her solution was to place a gauze pad between the hose and Rebekah's face to catch the water. (Our pediatrician later told us that you should never do such a thing for a baby with a heart condition.) We requested that the large, black hose be replaced, and we were certain that our request would be honored. We left for a few hours. When we returned, we found that not only had the hose not been replaced, but the constant dripping of water onto Rebekah's face had caused the entire side of her face to swell and her eyes to remain shut. Needless to say, at that moment all hell broke loose between these "overreacting" parents and the medical staff.

These were some of the instances of neglect and abuse that we feel our precious baby received while in that particular facility.

Even in the midst of times of darkness and despair, God always has His people. During these days of struggle, a wonderful clergywoman was a source of strength and comfort to us, and we will be forever grateful for her love and support. There are some people who seem to understand that the most important thing is just to be there. This lady knew that we just needed her compassion, not pity, and her loving presence to encourage and strengthen us. She was completely different from one hospital chaplain who had a loud mouth and would rattle off biblical quick fixes and phrases that would make my skin crawl. He tried to offer us a Band-Aid to put over a gaping hole. Whenever I heard his voice as he came down the hall, I would dread the encounter.

But God always knows what we need, so He sent the clergywoman.

We would be standing by my Becky's bedside and very quietly we would realize that she was there—just standing with us. She didn't try to offer platitudes; nor did she offer quick fixes, for she knew there were none. She would put her arms gently on our shoulders and just be there with us. She will never know what her presence did for us in those difficult times.

Rebekah remained in this hospital on the respirator for another four weeks until all of the money allotted for her heart surgery was exhausted. It struck us as quite a coincidence that her funds ran out at the same time that she was to be admitted at the other hospital for her heart surgery. When she was finally released, she was air-lifted to that hospital.As they prepared her for the flight, they let us see her and that picture I will never forget. The beautiful little girl so full of love for her family, loving her big sister and so freely giving of her love now frail, so weak scared from needle punctures and backed up IV lines. Her beautiful blonde hair shaved off for IV placements. Little hands that had once grasped our fingers, now almost skeleton like retracting from fear of more needle punctures. For her every touch now was a touch of pain. She looked longingly into my eyes. I couldn't help, I couldn't even hold her, and: I couldn't even touch her through the glass. Through her gaze I could hear her cry for help, her confusion of her situation. Where was her room with her soft toys and pretty blankets? Where were the soothing sounds of the songs sung to her in the night? How could she all of a sudden be taken from all of the beauty and comfort of her world and placed in such a place? Why were the two people in the world that loved her so much being separated from her by this dome of glass to never again experience the warmth and joy of home and family without pain and suffering?"

We were so helpless. We couldn't rescue our baby girl. We could only watch as they loaded Rebekah's frail little body onto the helicopter and took her away to a place that we thought would offer safety and help. We breathed easier now, knowing that she was free from this mistake-laden place and on her way to the help she needed. All she ever needed was to have her heart fixed.

Chapter 3

The Journey Begins

In Him we were also chosen, having been predestined according to the plan of Him who works out everything in conformity with the purpose of His will (Ephesians 1:11).

The will of God will never take you where the grace of God will not protect you.

On the two-and-a-half-hour drive to the new hospital, Frank and I gathered our thoughts and our hopefulness; we prepared to receive good news upon arrival at the place that would fix everything.

At the time, Frank's construction business was doing OK. He received a call on the way to the hospital about a new account, which changed our financial situation completely. The account would bring us to a new level of financial stability.

God seemed to be saying to us, "Because of the journey that you are beginning and the pressure that will be involved, I'm going to make sure that you don't have to worry about money. " And starting with that phone call, Frank's business prospered; money was always there for whatever we needed, so that was one pressure that we didn't have to worry about.

When we got to the hospital late that night, it was dark, cold, and raining. Arrangements had been made for us to stay at the Ronald McDonald House. At the hospital, we were directed to a room where the physician who had received her in the emergency room from the airlift flight, proceeded to inform us of her condition. The physician told us that Rebekah was in a greatly weakened condition and would have to be brought back to a healthier state for them to consider the surgery.

Rebekah's temperature was up, and she had had a seizure during the flight. We had asked that she be sedated for the flight, because she was very aware of her surroundings; we knew that she would be upset from the noise and movement of the helicopter. She was not given a sedative; again, we were ignored. I truly believe that had she been sedated, she would have made the trip without incident. But after all, she was "just" a baby with Down syndrome.

The plan was to get Rebekah nourished, raise her level of health, locate the cause of the fever, repair her heart, and send us home. It sounded like a plan that would work.

Frank and I checked into the Ronald Donald House late that night; we were cold, wet, and overwhelmed with the facts we had just been given. The house and its manager, Faye, wrapped us in love and warmth and a sense of refuge.

I thought of the scripture's exhortation to "give a cup of cold water in My name." In the midst of our confusion and helplessness, there was an oasis—a home away from home, a friend, and a family of parents walking through similar circumstances. We would bond with these people in a way that no other relationship can compare. We were comrades fighting for the lives and health of our children. It didn't matter who we were or where we were from; all that mattered was that we were fighting for the same cause.

I settled into my life at the McDonald House, Frank went home to work to keep the money coming in, my mom and dad took Miranda home with them, and Becky and I began our journey. Our little family separated in three different directions.

Frank would come to visit us on the weekends and he was always conflicted about the trip. He was excited to see Becky and me, but he struggled with the environment that he would walk into. As our elevator stopped on her floor and the door opened, his knees would buckle as he breathed in the air of this different world that required so much more of him than he could give. He had always been able to take care of us, to provide the wisdom and direction we needed, but he felt totally inadequate for his role in this arena.

We lived in separate worlds now. For me, it was hospitals and doctors and a little room at the Ronald McDonald House. I was in for the fight of my life. For Frank, a house that had once been filled with family, love, and laughter was now empty and painfully quiet. He missed tucking Miranda into bed, reading her a bedtime story, and sweet smells coming from the kitchen.

We were living in two different worlds, but with the same goal: to keep our little family safe and to be together once again.

I can't even imagine what thoughts coursed through Miranda's mind. At four years old, she was taken from her home and unable to feel her mother's touch. Yes, she was loved and secure with her grandparents, but still I wondered how a four-year-old could deal with her mother's absence.

My mother told me that there were times when Miranda would cry and say that she would never see her mother again. Mom and Dad would bring her to visit us, but she would be heartbroken when it was time to leave. There was no way she could understand that I, too, felt the same fear and grief over not being there for her.

My life was very routine. I would take the shuttle bus to the hospital by 8:00 a.m. and be by Rebekah's side in the ICU until 10:00 p.m. at night, go back to the RMH to get some sleep, and come back to the ICU the next day.

The constant drawing of blood and the burns resulting from backed-up IV lines left Rebekah with scars that never faded. The staff administered test after test, but they were unable to discover a reason for her fever. On one occasion they worked on her, fully conscious, for forty-five minutes to try to insert an arterial line, because it was so hard to find new veins for IVs; even so, their attempts were unsuccessful.

I walked to Rebekah's bed after this procedure and found it hard to believe that there was a baby in the bed. There was so much blood that it looked like an animal sacrifice had taken place. I was asked to try and calm Rebekah down, since she would always respond to my voice.

Two weeks of trying to improve Rebekah's health for heart surgery went by. Then one day, my mom and dad brought Miranda to visit me. Mom went to the hospital around 7:00 a.m., before the doctors made their rounds. She returned quickly and told me she thought Rebekah was in trouble. By the time I got there, an entire team of cardiologists, pediatricians, infectious-disease doctors, and residents had examined her. I had known that Rebekah was in trouble, and I wondered how the doctors could not have seen.

Becky was retracting vigorously, meaning that, even though she was still on a respirator, her heart and lungs were failing. I tried to calm her, but it didn't help. She would always respond to my voice and my touch, but not this time. The nurse came to suction her endotracheal tube, so I backed up against the wall on a small stool and watched. My eyes were glued to the heart monitor as the nurse disconnected Becky from the respirator and began to bag her manually.

The numbers on the heart monitor read, "206, 196, 97...0, Code Blue"; she had gone into cardiac arrest. Staff from all over the hospital emerged at her side in a matter of seconds. It was a whirlwind of activity; every person had a job and was doing it. Becky's potassium had gone too high. Her heart stopped for fifteen minutes, and it took a total of twenty minutes to get it started again. They had had to give her drugs to bring down her potassium level before they could get the heart beating again.

I waited in the hallway, pressed to the wall, feeling numb, alone, and helpless, like I was the only person on the planet. How can you pray with lips that are paralyzed and a body petrified like a piece of wood? You start from the inside. On the inside my spirit rose to the occasion and began to commune with my God. The kind of grace that God gives in moments like these cannot be explained. His grace envelopes and enables you to breathe, speak, and move. Without His grace, I felt as though I would have been a permanent part of the wall where I stood.

Staff came to get me, and explained, "There is a fine line with potassium." Too little or too much can have the same effect upon the body. Rebekah had been receiving potassium from several different sources. My questions remain unanswered: Why was the potassium level not monitored more closely? Why did the team of experts not see what was happening only an hour earlier? How did Rebekah's grandmother and mother see that something was wrong, but they didn't?

They tried to warn me before I returned to Becky's

bedside that the drugs they had to give her to bring the potassium level down had made her body swell. Nothing they said, however, could have prepared me for the picture that is imprinted in my mind to this day.

I walked up to her bedside, and she turned to see me. It was probably the last time she would see my face clearly, and those eyes that could see into your soul looked into mine. It was the most powerless and helpless moment of my life. I could do nothing, I couldn't take her and run, and I couldn't throw her a lifeline and draw her to safety. I was helpless and so was she laying there, a victim of such tragedy.

Her little body was swollen. Her head and neck were so large that it was hard to recognize her, but for those eyes. It was like she was trying to let me know that she knew it was not my fault. I gazed into those eyes of love as long as she was fully conscious and knew me. It would be our last moments of fully comprehending each other's presence and love with all of her faculties intact. It was the last time that she would see the love in her mother's eyes.

Grace Moments

It was only through God's grace that I could survive the depth of pain, disappointment, and grief that I felt at that moment. I was in a type of darkness that floods the soul, that eclipses all light, and that takes with it all hope of life beyond the moment. We are told that the human body can stay alive for three minutes without air, but the darkness is impossible to survive. But God comes into our darkness; He knows what we can bear, and He always comes.

For You are my lamp, O Lord; the Lord shall enlighten my darkness. For by You I can run against a troop; by my God I can leap over a wall (2 Samuel 22:29).

Some tests were run, and at first they showed no indication of brain damage. What a relief. But days later, an ultrasound revealed a tremendous amount of brain damage, and that Rebekah was having seizures.

Mom, Dad, and Miranda had gone home, and I was there all alone the day they told me that my precious baby girl had severe brain damage. I couldn't breathe. All I knew was that I had to get out of there, because the world was caving in on me.

I ran all the way to the Ronald McDonald House, praying all the way that I wouldn't have to see or speak to anyone. I made it to my room, fell into the bed, and pulled the covers over my head. I wanted the earth to open up and swallow me, as I was in the deepest, darkest place imaginable. My heart was bursting with pain, and I was alone, helpless, and hopeless. Death would be a welcome friend. I did not have the strength to pray. I wanted my heart to stop. How could it keep beating? How could a human heart bear this pain? I wanted my lungs to not take in another breath of air.How could someone live another moment after hearing such news?

Then, after what seemed to be an eternity, something

happened. Straight from the heart of God came His grace. I cannot explain how it came; it just came. Suddenly I had strength, clarity of thought and purpose, direction, and most of all, the presence of God or an angel or Jesus Himself, turning me into a warrior.

I shot straight up in bed, threw off the covers, and proclaimed with a loud voice, "No, we're not finished yet." I washed my face and I sang as I marched back to the hospital, "God's got an army marching through the land; deliverance is their song and healing in their hands, everlasting joy and peace down in their hearts, for in this army I've got a part." For the rest of Rebekah's stay there, I stood guard by her bedside with the strength of a century, protecting her, filtering every lab request (refusing those that were over the line), determined to allow only those things that my heart confirmed as good for her ongoing health.

Frank always says to me, "You never know what a day may bring. The dawning of one sun can change your life forever." We never know how close we are to a moment in time that seems far beyond our ability to survive. But this I know, God's grace comes. Grace is God doing for and through us what we cannot do or deserve.

Chapter 4

Quality of Life

So God created human beings in His own image. In the image of God He created them; male and female He created them (Genesis 1:227 NLT)

I was told that Rebekah would be given a loading dose of phenobarbital to bring her seizures under control. No one explained to me what a loading dose of phenobarbital would do or how it would affect Rebekah.

The next time I saw her she looked to be in a comatose state. I was led to believe that this was how she would remain for the rest of her life. Doctors took this opportunity to try to convince us to remove her life support. If we released her now, it would be over—case closed.

By this time a new team of doctors were in charge. Now her heart surgery was out of the question. Before she had only had Down syndrome, now she had severe brain damage, and a battle ensued over her life. We were bombarded with recommendations by doctors to withdraw life support and let Rebekah go (after all, a medical oversight needed to be covered up).

I truly believe that if I thought that Rebekah had been brain-dead, we would have had the grace to let her go. But something kept telling me that she was in there, that she would wake up. And she did.

The seizures continued, she lost her ability to eat, and she was diagnosed with cortical blindness. Her eyes were fine, but the part of the brain that registers sight was damaged. She would spend the rest of her life in the shadows.

In our fight for Rebekah's life, we were alone and confused, desperately searching for a ray of light in this darkness. Once we were given Rebekah's prognosis, it seemed that everyone around us began to distance themselves. People became emotionally detached, as if they knew where this road would end and had decided that we should be on our own. No one wants to go there; no one wants to be part of the end.

The medical staff who once were encouragers now seemed to become onlookers. At one time, they had been supportive, but now they left us on our own to whatever source of strength we might turn to. At times like these, some people turn to alcohol and drugs; and some retreat

mentally, thinking that what they don't acknowledge won't happen. But this was real, and it definitely was happening to us; we put our hope in God and Him alone. If He didn't help, there was no help.

Yes, we were all alone.

But God did what He always does—He came, He sent His representatives, and He sent help.

Help came in the form of Dr. E, a third-year resident. A pediatric cardiologist, Dr. E. was small in stature and unassuming in appearance; and he would come along and fight for our cause. We now faced the argument that, because Rebekah was brain-damaged and had no possibility of a quality life, it would be a waste of time, money, and effort to perform heart surgery on her.

The main cardiac doctor on the new team took me into a small room and placed a form before me for my signature. He communicated to me that my signature on the form would allow him to not give Rebekah any assistance should she "get into trouble" in the night. I not only did not sign the form, but explained to the seven-foot-tall doctor that neither he nor I had enough deity to determine who lives or dies. If Rebekah were to "get into trouble" at any time of day or night, the doctor was to do all in his power to help her. I was certain that if I signed the form, Rebekah would "get into trouble" in my absence.

Doctor E. spent much time with me, in order to understand us and our values. He spent much time with Rebekah, too, in order to assess her overall condition.

The argument against her surgery was that even if the surgery were done, Rebekah still would not be able to come off the ventilator because of her brain damage. Doctor E. believed that she would, and he even went to the ICU late one night and took her off by himself, just to see how she would respond. He was fully convinced that she should have the surgery and be restored to her family.

I will never forget the last meeting that we had with the team of experts. We sat at a large conference table with neurologists, cardiologists, infectious-disease doctors, and our third-year-resident pediatric cardiologist. Everyone but Dr. E. stated that if we chose to let Rebekah live, our lives would be hell, Miranda would hate her sister, and Frank and I would divorce. If Rebekah lived, she would take, take, take, and our lives would be over. Besides, they said, she would never come off the ventilator.

Dr. E. stood against them all, gave his assessment of Rebekah, and told them to fix her heart. He maintained that Rebekah would come off the respirator and go home.

At one point during the meeting, the main cardiologist advised us to withdraw life support and let Becky go. Frank inquired as to what would happen when the respirator was removed. The doctor explained that her lungs would fill with fluid and that she would die. In reality, she would drown. Frank asked how long it would take, and the doctor replied three days. So his recommendation was that we withdraw life support, stand by her bed for three days, and watch her slowly drown.

Unable to comprehend what we were hearing, Frank responded sarcastically, "Well, doc, can't you give her a shot of something to make it happen quicker?" For a moment, the doctor actually pondered the possibility.

After much debate, the team of doctors finally honored our request for her surgery. The day before the surgery, we met with the surgeon who would perform the operation. He looked at us and said these words, "It doesn't do my ego any good to operate on a baby like yours. I'll probably kill her on the table. Just so you two can go through the rest of your lives knowing that you did all that you could, I'll do it."

My husband responded, "Well, doctor, it has been my and Brenda's experience that when we come to a door in life, we just keep on walking through the door until there are no more doors to walk through. We're going to walk through this one. Now, you just do your job, and do it well."

The next day, Rebekah had her heart surgery and, in the surgeon's words, "sailed through it. " The surgeon was amazed and pleased and had a complete change of attitude. In three days, Rebekah came off the respirator; all tubes were removed also, to everyone's amazement.

I wondered many times if Dr. E. had any idea that almighty God had used him to stand against a Goliath, as

David the shepherd did, and rescue a helpless little girl.

Rebekah's health began to rapidly improve; but she was not able to eat on her own, so we allowed the placement of a feeding tube. A G-tube (gastrointestinal tube) was surgically inserted through her stomach wall and attached to the stomach so that we would be able to pour liquid nourishment directly into the stomach. Whatever it took to get her out and home, we told ourselves. We would deal with that later.

As Frank and I were making preparations to bring Rebekah home, my parents waited in her room. The new team head accosted Mom and Dad with his evaluation of the situation. He very graphically laid out his view of Rebekah's condition and told them that we were unwise (not his choice of words) to even consider bringing this child into our home. As you can imagine, Mom and Dad, who were so excited that we were on the other side of this ordeal, now felt blasted with negativity. Yes, we knew exactly what we were getting into (they had made it more than crystal clear), but it was our choice. The soldier in my dad rose up, and he informed the new team leader in no uncertain terms of the value of this child, who had a name and was part of the family who loved her. He said, "Doctor, as for Rebekah's care, this little granny [pointing to my mother] and I have nothing better to do for the rest of our lives, but to take care of this precious girl. We love her and count it our joy and privilege to do whatever she needs for the rest of our lives."

So on March 28, 1986, after her seven-month hospital stay on a ventilator, we brought our little girl home.

Chapter 5

Realizing What Was Lost

And God is able to make all grace abound toward you, that you always having all sufficiency in all things, may have an abundance for every good work (2 Corinthians 9:8).

While you are fighting for a life in the hospital, the gravity of the situation does not become clear until sometime later. After we got Rebekah home, we began to see how much of her we had lost. The precious smile that once filled our heart with joy was now gone. I thought it had to be temporary; her smile was too much to lose. But it was gone forever; it was taken from her.

As I began to realize how much of her was lost, I grieved to the very core of my being. The next months would amount to a continual death and burial of aspects of her that we would never get back. She was there, but not there.

The words "how" and "why" began to fill my mind. How could God have allowed this to happen to my baby? He wasn't on vacation; His head wasn't turned. He could have prevented this, but He didn't. I felt like I was trying to put a round peg into a square hole; I just couldn't get it to fit.

The formula that was put into Rebekah's G-tube caused her pain. Her bowel movements were laborious. She had do exercises to relieve the stomach pain, which increased and took over her life. The days were filled with trying to relieve the pain. Rebekah slept very little and found no joy. There was no normal life; everything had changed. Days and nights ran together and became one continual nightmare.

Mom and Dad came to stay with us during the week and would go home on weekends. My mother slept on a pallet next to Rebekah's bed for a year, while my dad slept on a cot in the living room. Later, permanent arrangements were made for them. Every effort was for survival. There was nothing that even resembled a normal life. Our days were filled with trying to relieve Rebekah's pain and managing the stress of dealing with a brain-damaged and now blind child. I also wondered how I would maintain my own sanity and the well-being of my husband and Miranda.

Since Cortical blindness was part of Rebekah's

diagnosis, she not only suffered with intense intestinal pain, seizures, and a feeding tube, but also with the fear that accompanied her darkness. Still, she was very much intact on the inside. If she had been simply a physical body with no emotional connections or thought processes, everything would have been much simpler. But she was very present and had unique ways to communicate what was going on inside.

A combination of my awareness of what Rebekah had lost and my mounting internal question of how and why the loss had occurred brought me to a place of mental and emotional breakdown. Our little family was fighting to survive like never before. I anguished over the sentence that had been pronounced on all of us. Rebekah was the one in chains, but we were all held captive in her prison. Miranda was losing her mother. There were no more tea parties, no baking cookies, and no more snuggling on the sofa to watch a favorite movie. I was not free to be what I had been to Miranda. The intimate moments with her were few, if any. Luckily she allowed her dad to step into the role that I had cherished with her only months before. How could she possibly understand the reversal, the pain, the uncertainty? What future would this four-year-old have without her mother?

It seemed that pressure and stress increased by the minute. Darkness filled our lives; a dark-gray haze seemed to fill the atmosphere of our home. How much pressure and uncertainty could we withstand? I realized that not only was Rebekah bound and trapped, but, barring a miracle, I was bound and trapped as well. My life was over. I was bound to a rocking chair with a screaming baby, and my fate was sealed. Life was going on without me; outside, the seasons were changing, but mine remained the same.

Frank realized the seriousness of my mental condition and made arrangements for me to go to Christian Retreat in Bradenton, Florida. He told me that I had to get alone with God. My mother and dad would take care of Rebekah, and he would take care of Miranda. I didn't argue; I knew that I had to hear from God. I would not be able to go on without some understanding. So I packed my bag, climbed into Frank's work van, and drove to Bradenton.

I will never forget the moment that I walked through the door of my room. The presence of God had gone before me and was waiting. Frank had flowers waiting for me there, but they paled to the voice of God waiting and ready for my questions. Questions that now in His presence seemed secondary. The love and grace of God enveloped me. The atmosphere was filled with the same hushed but holy reality that had so marked Rebekah's birth.

How do you conduct yourself in this presence of God? Do you speak or keep quiet? I had so much to say and so many questions, and at the same time, it didn't seem to matter. It seemed as though I didn't have to ask my questions, because the cry of my heart had already reached heaven.

I didn't get all of the answers that I came for that day, but God talked to me. He had to set my feet on solid ground. I stayed at Christian Retreat for four days. I lived in that presence for four days and let His voice bring healing to my broken heart and strength to my mind, spirit, and body for the journey that lay ahead, one that would change my life forever. Little did I know that this brain-damaged, blind little girl had so much to teach me about God and His ways. She was trapped in a body full of pain, but she spoke eternal truth to those around her.

The foundational truth that He shared with me was that I had brought His character into question. I had sinned when I put a question mark on God's character by asking, "How could God have allowed this to happen to my baby?" Sin separates us from God, and when we are separated from God, we die. I was definitely dying. I had been cut off from my life source; I was separated from His fellowship, voice, and grace.

God is just in all His ways and kind in all His doings (Psalm 145:17).

Even when I don't understand, when it doesn't add up or make sense to me, the fact remains that God is just and kind. He makes no mistakes, and His love is sure. I was the one with the problem; I was the one who had to get aligned with truth. It meant my very survival.

Over the course of those few days, God made the truth of His "just and right" ways so much a part of my life that it has become one of the cornerstones of my life and walk with Him. The knowledge of this aspect of His character is foundational to all of life. We can count on truth to guide us safely through uncertainty. When we can't see past dark clouds or hear above crashing waves, He remains the same—just and kind and present.

There were many painful happenings, particularly at the first hospital, that to recall them brought me intense pain. The Lord in His goodness had me bring up each painful picture in my mind and, as an act of my will, forgive the person who created the pain. Forgiveness is never for the sake of those forgiven; it is for those who must forgive. We cannot afford to allow unforgiveness to remain in our hearts. It will grow, overtake us, and eventually take our lives. Forgiveness is not a feeling or an emotion; instead, it is a decision that we make to let something go even before we have any idea of what the outcome will be. To forgive is not to say that what people did or did not do was OK, nor does it set them free from their wrongdoing; it simply allows God to be the one to make adjustments. So one by one I brought up the horrible pictures in my mind, and, out loud, I forgave those who had wronged us, releasing them and what they did to the Lord. That day God set me free from the awful pain I was carrying. Since then, my recollections of those particular situations do not bring me pain. Forgiveness sets us free so that we can be healed.

I returned home to face the same pressures that I had left, but now I had the proper understanding of how to deal with and process the situations that lay ahead. For two more years, pressure would increase and bring about more and more areas of struggle for survival.

Where I went from there depended on where I went with questions. God is a loving God and doesn't mind our questions; but when our questions lead us to wrong conclusions, we are in trouble. When our questions bring the love and goodness of God into question, we are in trouble. A question like "If God were a God of love, then why did He let this happen?" leads to a wrong conclusion. I completely understood the justice of God, that He doesn't make mistakes and everything He does is kind and good. I was overwhelmed by trying to reckon the character of God with my present circumstances. It was like trying to mix oil and water or night and day or good and evil. It was constantly tearing at my mind, moment by moment, day by day.

In every situation of life we have a window of opportunity, in which we are given a moment in time to evaluate and calculate our destiny. In that moment, time seems to stand still as we decide on which direction we will take. We have the opportunity to make the choice— hopefully, the right choice—that will set the course of our journey.

And hopefully we have come to know God to be loving, kind, just, long-suffering, and true, and to know that whatever comes our way is for our ultimate good, and will serve to make us better people. Learning to recognize these windows of opportunity is invaluable to living a victorious Christian life.

In those moments we draw from our well of understanding of God and His ways, and hopefully we choose to stand on His Word in Romans 8:28: "And we know that all things work together for good to those who love God, to those who are called according to His purpose."

Most of the time, we have a spiritual understanding of this scripture. But when devastating situations arise, the logical and emotional parts of our being cause complete chaos. The hows and whys and the whos kick in and overpower the truth that brought us comfort in the past.

There were many times in my journey that "everything" I believed was challenged. We have to realize that this is how it works. We are human and frail and when bad things happen to ones we love our humanity kicks in, but we don't have to stay there. When we get knocked off of our place of confidence, we allow God's truth to be our equalizer.

The struggle to reconcile the truth with our circumstances is mammoth, and some people never make it through. Some people spend their entire lives with the question "Why?" branded in their mind and heart, unable to move forward to the other side of pain. And there is another side of pain, for no suffering lasts forever when our perspective is right. It comes to an end, and in its place are joy and freedom and a greater understanding of the love of our God.

When we make the right choice in our window of opportunity, it enables us to become better and not bitter.

Chapter 6

Someone Tell Me I Will Survive

Weeping may endure for a night, but joy comes in the morning (Psalm 30:5).

During this period of time, Rebekah slept for only an hour and a half at a time, in between bouts of pain. I never slept through the night. Whenever I would go to the store, I would look at people and think to myself, "I wonder how much time they get to sleep. " I would longingly remember earlier days when we had a normal life and I would get to sleep through the night without having a baby screaming with pain. Now my mother and I were working all hours of the night, trying to relieve Becky's pain.

I found myself in the nursery rocking chair, gazing out the window, watching the world go by, watching the seasons change, wondering if I would ever be part of the world outside again. I was totally isolated!

My heart breaks when I think of the many people who are now sitting in the place where I was—in a chair, in a room, held captive by a heartbreaking situation. I think of their crippled bodies and broken minds, of all kinds of diseases that take the very life out of a relationship or a family. I think of people who are housebound and at the same time bound to stress and pressure and agony in their hearts and souls. Whys and hows are flooding their minds as they search to find someone to tell them that they can survive the awful injustices of life.

I want each and every one of these precious ones to know that, yes, I have been there and know that you can survive. You can make it through and come out on the other side, better and unbroken.

The questions that arise from our pain are Where is God, and does He care? Yes, He cares and He is there for everyone who will call upon Him and invite His presence and power into their situation.

There are many questions that we will not have an answer for until we get to heaven, but this I know: God is good, and He does good.

I had always been able to fix my circumstances, to change my surroundings to fit whatever I wanted, but not now—not this time. When you are the mother, the buck stops here. There was finally something in my life that I couldn't change, couldn't fix, or couldn't run from. The pressure was real, the looming destruction to my marriage and little family was real. Frank and I could no longer meet each other's needs, the pressure was dividing us and we no longer even knew each other. We lived in two different worlds. He went to work each day trying to keep our finances afloat and would return home to a house of stress and pressure that he felt responsible for, but was totally unable to resolve. I, on the other hand, had looked around at the areas of stress in my life; I knew that Miranda and Rebekah were my children and I couldn't do anything about that, but Frank could be eliminated from the picture.

Stress will bring divisiveness in a marriage and destroy a family, unless a husband and a wife are determined to cleave to each other. We had been living in separate worlds for so long that it was easier to turn from each other than to cleave to each other; too much had pulled us apart already. We were fighting merely for self-preservation; we just wanted to survive. God's anointing and provision come to those who can stay in a place of unity as husband and wife. If the enemy (Satan) or their circumstances can separate them, then they continue to move farther and farther apart. Couples who were once madly in love can find themselves living together as strangers, with all feelings of love and commitment fading somewhere into the past.

The doctors had told us that if we chose to allow Rebekah to live, she would destroy us. The pressure from this child would destroy our marriage, and Miranda would hate her. These facts were true, except that the doctors failed to factor in the "But God..." element. The enemy may intend everything to be for our harm; but God uses things that are meant to destroy us in order to refine us and make us better, so long as we yield to Him.

Only through God's amazing grace did Frank and I realize what was happening, and we made a decision to not allow our circumstances to destroy us. We realized that God would somehow restore our relationship if we made the right choices. So we turned back toward each other and gradually, sometimes moment by moment, fought our way back to a place of unity where we could once again cleave to each other.

One of the many things that I have learned is that pressure is always designed for a purpose. I didn't have a clue at the time, but God's purpose in my life was to set me free from my self-sufficiency—He wanted me to know His love—so that I would be able to trust Him. God wanted to see His reflection in my life, but I was too filled with self, doing everything in my own strength and in my own way.

There was a story told of someone who visited a refiner of silver. They watched as the refiner placed the precious metal into a pot and turned up the fire. The refiner never took his eyes from the pot and was constantly monitoring the process. There were times when he had to turn up the heat, but he was always in control of the heat and its effect on the precious metal. As the process continued there came a time when waste materials would come to the top, so the refiner would scoop them off and discard them. When the process was finished, there was a purified piece of flawless silver. The person watching asked the refiner, "How do you know when the process is complete?" and the refiner replied, "When I can see my reflection in the pot."

Sometimes God has to turn up the heat so that He can remove the impurities from our lives. Attitudes and behavior that aren't pleasing to Him or are harmful to us and others. He is always in control of the heat and is always monitoring our progress. He is like the refiner looking to see His reflection in our lives.

God certainly wanted to see His reflection in my life. There were many nights when Mother and I would be up at 1:00 a.m., trying over the next couple of hours to relieve Rebekah's pain. I remember nights when I faced the pain and screaming alone, tried everything I knew to relieve her pain, but found that nothing worked. I prayed for God's help, I begged for His help, but there was none. The heavens were brass, a scriptural term meaning God's voice was not heard, not even a whisper. I would look up to heaven, and in a not-so-kind voice ask, "Why don't You do something?"

There was no still small voice that said, "Everything's going to be all right." There was nothing; but I didn't realize that, in the midst of the nothingness, a greater purpose was at work.

Little did I know that the pressure I felt was to set me free from the self-sufficient, self-reliant chains that had me bound. I thought the pressure would destroy me, but instead it would ultimately set me free. But for the moment, all I knew was that my life was over; apart from a miracle, there was no hope. I would be trapped forever in this chair, with this child, in this room with its walls.

I searched diligently for someone to just tell me that I could survive this, that they had been in that same place and survived. I cried, "Someone please tell me that I can survive." I didn't know then that no suffering lasts forever, that an end would come, and we could move past this season to a place of sunshine again. I didn't know that there was something very powerful at work in our little family.

One night I fell into bed and Frank wrapped me up in his arms, and I asked him to tell me that we were going to make it, that we could survive this. He replied, "Brenda, who wins the prizefight in a boxing match?" I didn't exactly know the answer, so he said, "It is the one who keeps coming out for one more round. Can you come out for one more round? Can you get up and go on for just one more day? I know that you can't imagine that you can go the entire fifteen rounds, but can you just get up and come out for one more day?" I thought for a moment and knew that, yes, I could come out one more time. I could by God's grace do one more day. He said, "Then that is all you have to do—just come out one more day. Each day you just come out one more time, and one day that will be the last time and it will be over." So I stopped thinking of the future and how totally impossible our lives were. I only had to come out one more time. Each night I would close the door on that day and allow God to give me the grace to come out for one more round. He remained faithful and provided the grace for each new day. There is no way to explain how we survived except by His grace, by Him doing in us and through us what was impossible for us to do on our own. Impossible situations require a grace that is far beyond ourselves.

The apostle Paul said:

> *Yet what we suffer now is nothing compared to the glory He will reveal to us later (Romans 8:18 NLT).*

Beyond our struggle and suffering there would come a day when the glory of God, through our journey with Him who means all things ultimately for our good, would be revealed.

Chapter 7

Surrender

Or do you not know that your body is the
temple of the Holy Spirit who is in you,
whom you have from God, and you are not
your own? For you were bought at a price,
therefore glorify God in your body and in
your spirit, which are God's (1 Corinthians
6:19–20).

By this time two years had passed and the struggle had taken its toll. My marriage was holding together by a thread. Miranda did not understand that the struggle was not Rebekah's fault, and her love for her sister had turned to anger. Anything that you could think of that normal families do, we didn't. Frank and I were just trying to hold it all together. The only time I left the house was to buy groceries and go to the bank on Fridays. There were no outings, no fun, and no recreation. Our situation threatened to rip us apart, but God's grace kept us together.

Mom and Dad had gone home on this particular weekend, which meant that I had to care for Rebekah by myself. Frank could help, but he had his hands full with the meals, Miranda's care, and anything else around the house that was needed. The weekends were horrible. I had to hold Becky all of the time. She did not have behavior issues; she was very much intact mentally and emotionally. But she was blind and just couldn't make connections between her brain and her body. The older she got, the more aware of her bondage she became. We held her for her security and comfort. We had tried therapy, but it didn't work; it only served to torment her. We dealt with bouts of pneumonia, doctors' misdiagnoses, teeth crumbling due to high doses of antibiotics, and many other issues that figured in the care of a handicapped child like Rebekah.

I struggled with all that was required of me to care for Rebekah. My mom could sit in her rocking chair for hours upon hours, singing and praying. It never seemed to bother her that she had been taken from her world. Mom and Dad were ready to give the rest of their lives just to help us care for Rebekah. I, on the other hand, found it very hard to stay in the chair hour after hour. My mind would fill with all of the things that I would never be able to do again and all of the things that I couldn't do now. I was a wife and a mother and I wasn't able to do any of the things that go along with those roles. I hated my feelings; I hated the struggle inside. I wanted to care for my child, but at the same time I wanted my life back. I didn't want my mom and dad to have to help us; I wanted to take care of my family. I wanted to be able to run my household again, do Mommy things with Miranda, and be a wife to Frank. But there was Rebekah. It was an ongoing struggle knowing that I was doing the perfect will of God, but having to depend on His grace moment by moment.

On that Sunday morning, Frank said, "Why don't you go to church today? I think I can take care of Rebekah, so you go." I never was able to go to church, and did not consider myself spiritually minded at that time. The journey has a way of wearing you down, but the thought appealed to me for some reason.

I found a seat about halfway in and on the right side of the church. I can't tell you what the pastor preached about or what songs the congregation sang that morning, but I can tell you exactly what God said to me.

As the service progressed, I was filled with anguish of heart and confusion. I had gone as far as I could go in my present condition. I looked up toward heaven, and in a not-so-nice voice, I asked the $64,000 question: "What do You want from me?" I know that everyone in heaven must have risen to their feet. I had reached a place where what He wanted didn't matter anymore; He could have it. If He wanted my arm, He could take it; if He wanted my leg, He could cut it off. Whatever the issue was, I was ready to settle it. I couldn't go on; God had to do something.

No sooner did I ask the question than the answer came quickly and clearly. He said, "I want you to surrender. I want your whole heart, not part of it, but all of it." Lordship isn't about halfheartedness; it's about giving Him 100 percent of our being. After all, God gave the best He had, His only Son Jesus Christ, who in turn gave His all on Calvary. His sacrifice for us was total, so our commitment to Him must be our whole heart.

I didn't know what all was involved at that moment, but I knew that I must surrender my heart and life to the lordship of Christ. I gladly made my commitment to Christ that morning. I said, "Lord, I don't know what all it means, but I surrender my whole heart to You today. I hold nothing back; no area is off limits to You. I give it all to You and to Your lordship." In that moment it felt as though the weight of the world had lifted off my shoulders. I could breathe again—it seemed that the air became fresh and God's light filled my body and spirit.

I went home that day a free woman. I still had all of the same stresses in my life, but now I was free on the inside. I felt as though the chains that had been wrapped around and around me had been loosened, and a new day had begun.

Over the next few months God took me through a process of teaching me about His sovereignty, His lordship, my position in Him, and His in me. As I would take my morning walk, He would say to me, "Do you hear your heartbeat?"

"Yes, Lord," I would reply.

"Your heart does not beat another time except that I will it to beat. Do you feel your lungs take in air and exhale?"

"Yes, Lord."

"Your lungs do not take another breath except for the fact that I will it to be so. You are not your own, you've been bought with a price. You belong to Christ."

Over those months He brought me to the place where I said, "Lord, for the rest of my days, whatever Your will is for my life, the answer is yes. Before You even ask the question of me, the answer is yes."

For whoever desires to save his life will lose it, but whoever loses his life for My sake will find it (Matthew 16:25).

The words "surrender" and "submission" are not popular words these days. Very seldom do you hear any of the television ministers speak on either of these topics.

The popular messages are about prosperity and "tying a need to a seed," and at the end of these messages, a dollar amount is always required to be able to enter into the promised "blessing." While I totally believe in God's promise of financial prosperity, I also believe that we can be so focused on gaining earthly riches that we miss out on His purpose for our lives.

Give yourselves to God...Surrender your

whole being to Him to be used for righteous purposes (Romans 6:13 Today's English Version [TEV]).

The word "surrender" makes one think of defeat, death, and a loss of one's identity. Quite the opposite is true. Only as we lose our lives in Him can we ever truly come to experience who we really are. He created us to our very core.

C. S. Lewis said, "The more we let God take us over, the more truly ourselves we become—because He made us...He invented all the different people that you and I were intended to be...It is when I turn to Christ, when I give up myself to His personality that I first begin to have a real personality of my own."

We give ourselves to Christ not because of some legal code, but out of love, "because He first loved us."

Somehow by losing our life to Him, we truly find life. Freedom from wanting to control/be in charge of our own lives enables God to come in and do in us and through us what we are totally incapable of doing on our own. Complete surrender of the self is not about losing something, it is about gaining everything. So why do we resist it so much? Imagine hanging from a small limb after falling from the edge of a mountain, and waiting for the arrival of a very large and powerful helicopter that has been sent for your rescue. The rescuer has been lowered from the helicopter to retrieve you and take you to a place of safety, but you must let go of your branch. Sometimes we can't seem to see beyond the things we are holding onto, to know that God has so much more to bring us into. A.W. Tozer said, "The reason why so many are still troubled, still seeking, still making little forward progress is because they haven't yet come to the end of themselves. We're still trying to give orders, and interfering with God's work within us. " Only God is God, we're not!

Being able to surrender or let go to God and His lordship requires an understanding of His great love for us, which results in our being able to trust Him. Without this knowledge we continue to rely on our own strengths and earthly wisdom.

Most of our struggle in life is with God; we want complete control. We will never win this battle.

I had lived my life with marginal lordship. Remember the words of the old song: "If He's not Lord of all, then He's not Lord at all. " He is never satisfied with even 95 percent; He wants all of us.

> *So then, my friends, because of God's great mercy to us...offer yourselves as a living sacrifice to God, dedicated to His service and pleasing to Him. This is the true worship that you should offer (Romans 12:1 TEV).*

This is our "reasonable service"—all of us. Romans 12:1

The characteristic of a surrendered life is obedience and trust.

Because we know Him (and His great love for us), we obey and trust Him even when we do not know the outcome.

We stop trying to manipulate people or situations.

We stop trying to force our own will.

We simply let go and let God do the work.

> *Surrender yourself to the Lord, and wait patiently for Him (Psalm 37:7 TEV).*

As a result:

Rick Warren in the *Purpose Driven Life* writes:

Peace comes. "Stop quarreling with God. If you agree with Him, you will have peace at last, and things will go well for you."

Freedom comes. "Offer yourselves to the ways of God and the freedom never quits...[His] commands set you free to live openly in His freedom."

God's power comes. "All of the overpowering struggles in our lives can be overcome by Christ's power when given to

Him" (Rick Warren, *The Purpose Driven Life*).

"Fullness of joy is discovered only in the emptying of will." (Ann Voskamp)

We must allow the arrival of that moment in time when we fully surrender all of ourselves to Christ, just as I did in church that morning, but we must also make daily, conscious decisions to live a surrendered life. The enemy will always challenge our decisions; but when we continue to make the right choices, God's power comes to enforce our commitment. Rick Warren said, "A living sacrifice can crawl off the altar at any time."

We don't have to be afraid. When God is in control, nothing is out of His control.

> Paul said, *"I am ready for anything and equal to anything through Him who infuses inner strength into me, that is, I am self-sufficient in Christ's sufficiency"* *(Philippians 4:13).*

What we hold onto we lose; but what we release to Him, He replaces with something much richer. Only in the kingdom of God does dying produce life. We fight so hard to save or preserve our lives, but only as we die to ourselves can Christ be made alive in us. Only as there is less of me can there be more of Him.

We choose daily to say no to ourselves and yes to Christ; we take up our cross daily. The cross is simply an intersection of wills. It is where our will intersects with the will of Christ. At that point something must die, and that is our will to His.

From the moment that I made that decision in church that day, everything changed. Rebekah's pain began to stop, she was left with only minor discomfort that needed a little assistance from us. She began to sleep through the night and a great sense of peace came to her.

My mother had worked with Rebekah to help her learn to eat again, and against the doctors' statements that she would never be able to eat or drink by mouth, Rebekah did. It was a glorious day when we had her G-tube removed and she stopped having seizures. She gradually moved to being able to eat baby cereal and even carrots. We fed her so many carrots (because she would eat them) that she turned orange.

We all worked together and each one had their own specialty with her. Mother and I were the bad guys when we had to exercise her and do the things that she didn't want done. My dad, Poppa to Rebekah, made up a little song; and whenever we would rough her up, as Poppa called it, he would scoop her up in her arms and sing, "It's Going to be All Right in the Middle of the Night. " She just loved it. We each had our own rocking chair that she preferred us to use. Wouldn't you know that mine was the old one that had been dropped off the back of a truck? It was held together with wire and nails and glue and made a horrible creaking sound, but that's where I sat to take care of her.

She didn't let very many people hold her, but she loved for Miranda to get in our old, blue swivel chair and swing her back and forth while singing to her whatever tune Miranda chose that day. She would stay in Miranda's lap as long as Miranda could confine herself to the chair— Miranda was a child on the go. Even with Rebekah's issues, she still loved her big sister.

Over the next months, Frank and I realized that "the gift and call of God is without repentance," and we knew that God's will for our lives had not changed, so we began to take the necessary steps to return to ministry. We had been to a meeting in Lakeland, Florida, where we were reinstated with our district, so that we could once again be considered for a pastoral leadership position in one of our denominational churches. On the ride home, we were aware of the Lord's presence and could sense that He was setting us back into the place of our calling. It was like a split occurred in the atmosphere, and we separated from an old something into a new something. A door was closed on the past as we entered into our destiny once again.

Frank and I had been fighting to reclaim the unity in our marriage, and little by little we had found our way back together. The thing that the enemy had wanted to use to destroy us became the thing that God used to make our marriage stronger than ever before. It is true that if we continue in God's Word with determination and are relentless with His principles, our destruction will turn into our victories and bring glory to God.

The second anniversary of bringing Rebekah home from the hospital came, and I remember standing in front of the mirror and flexing my muscles like a bodybuilder. I said, "It's been two years and we are still standing, two years and we're stronger than we've ever been. Two years and our marriage is stronger, our family is still together and we have an understanding of God and His ways that makes everything worth the price. " We had defied the odds; the doctors' words were true except for the "But God…" element. I felt like I had steel in my veins, although not in a cold and unbending way; I had been emptied of self and, in its place, God had come and filled me with Himself. I no longer was the strong-willed, self-sufficient person that I used to be; I had allowed Christ to free me from my will and replace it with His life. I felt like David, when he said,

> *He teaches my hands to make war, so that my arms can bend a bow of steel (2 Samuel 22:35).*

No one knew better than I that I was not adequate for my circumstances, but I had come to know without any doubt that "I can do all things through Christ who strengthens me." I not only can, but will survive and thrive.

We came to realize, like the three Hebrew children did, (Daniel 3:1-28) that when we are in "the fire of God," He comes. He comes into your fiery furnace and, if you let

Him, He will teach you how to have a song "in the fire." His presence will sustain you until He brings you out on the other side. The only things that will be consumed by the fire are the things that hold you captive: self-sufficiency and determination to do things your way and be Lord of your own life.

When God turns up the heat in our lives, it is not to harm us but only to free us. The pressure that is designed to break us will never crush us. God is kind and loving and only wants what He judges to be best for us. He loves us too much to leave us the way we are.

Chapter 8

The Cross

The Apostle Paul said, I die daily.

Jesus said, If anyone desires to come after Me, let him deny himself, and take up his cross, and follow Me. For whoever desires to save his life will lose it, but whoever loses his life for My sake will find it (Matthew 16:24–25 NLT)

We see crosses everywhere; they have become a popular piece of jewelry. They are varied in size and finish. You see large crosses covered with diamonds and layered among strands of chains from the necks of hip-hop singers. You see them pierced into various body parts, and (especially appalling to me) strategically placed to rest in the cleavage of a woman's exposed breasts.

Other crosses that I find painful to look at, even though they are used for religious purposes, are tall and show Jesus still nailed there for all to see. I know that image is supposed to be a sacred reminder, but Jesus is not still on the tree.

The cross is an instrument of freedom, not a frivolous decoration to be flaunted. It should be an honor to wear the symbol of our redemption and should signify one's commitment to follow Jesus.

Apart from the physical symbol of the cross, its spiritual significance applies to our everyday life. Dying daily to our own will as Jesus instructs us will always present a struggle.

My struggle was that I didn't want to be in that rocking chair. I wanted to be out on the other side of the window. I wanted to be going places and doing things. I wanted to be in the kitchen, leisurely making a special dinner for my family. I wanted to sit down in the evening and watch a television program or play a game with my family. I wanted to have a tea party with Miranda or go shopping for a new pair of shoes. I wanted to be the person I was before all of this began, and my fear was that I'd never be that person again.

It wasn't that I didn't love Rebekah; I would have laid down my life, literally, for her. I would have donated an organ or my blood—nothing from my physical body would have ever been too great a price. It was the price on the inside that caused the struggle that can be represented by the cross. The cross is an intersection of wills: my will and God's will.

The cross that Christ talked about was not a physical one; I didn't have to literally be put to death on it. It was that place where the perfect will of God intersected with my will. I knew in those moments of anguished struggle that God's perfect will for me was in my rocking chair with my daughter with no set date for a conclusion.

When our will intersects with God's will, our will must die. This is the cross. The struggle is real, the reality is, of course, real; but the freedom that comes as we make the right choice is also very real.

I must decrease in order for Him to increase:

> Emptiness itself can birth the fullness of grace because in the emptiness we have the opportunity to turn to God, the only begetter of grace, and there find all the fullness of joy.
>
> Suffering can deliver grace (Ann Voskamp).

Everything inside me wanted to jump up and run screaming, "No, no this isn't the way it's supposed to be, this can't be my fate." I know these words sound hard and uncaring, but they clarify the struggle that we have on the inside. It was never an issue of love, but one of the self: dying to desire for the basic joys of life.

Every morning as I awoke and faced a new day, I had to make a decision: do I live for myself today, or do I die to self and allow God's grace to enable me to walk in His will for my life? It is always our choice. We are never forced to submit to Christ's cross. But may God please deliver us from thinking that the only thing that matters is our present comfort.

I knew what dying to self meant. I knew it meant hours in the rocking chair, watching Rebekah scream with pain, in those earlier days, that I couldn't ease. I knew that the world outside would continue to pass me by, totally oblivious to what was going on behind the walls of our pretty little house.

To me, taking up the cross and dying daily means that there will come times in our lives when we, like the three Hebrew children, have to step into the fire. They knew that their God could deliver them; but they also knew that if He didn't, that would be OK too.

I'm certain that they didn't realize what was going to happen next. Their thoughts were that either they would be delivered or they would die.

But God had another plan with far more significance than they thought possible.

He came into the fire with them, so that the flames did not consume them but burned through their bonds. They experienced total freedom in the furnace, in the presence of the almighty God.

Again, when they came out of the furnace—remember, no suffering lasts forever—only the things that had held them captive were affected by the flames.

I'm sure that being thrown into a fiery furnace was not at the top of their to-do lists for that day. It definitely was not their desire or will, but it was obviously how God had planned to demonstrate His power to that generation and all that would follow.

There will come times in our lives when we will, in the perfect will and timing of the Lord, be called upon to step into the fire. That will be a point of intersection. Will we kick and scream like toddlers or blame God for not being there? Or will we, because we have practiced a daily dying to our own will, step into the fire knowing that God means all things for our good? Will we remember that the fire will not destroy us, but will purify our hearts so that a great reflection of Jesus will be seen in our lives? Remember that He comes into our fire, and we get to know Him in a way that no other experience can provide.

When we make the right choice as I had to each morning, of whose will I would follow, somehow His grace came every time. I'm still here, and I'm better than I was before. My three and a half years with Becky did not destroy me; they freed me to become the person God created me to be.

It was a dark day as Jesus was dying on the cross, and if it had ended there, it would have been tragic. But the cross was just the instrument that God used for a far greater purpose. The cross was just one part of His purpose. There was also the empty tomb and the salvation that was purchased for all mankind.

To every trial and every suffering, there is always "the other side," which is meant to reflect God's goodness. Jesus Himself was an example to us of the inner struggle of the cross when He was in the garden. He knew that what was before him was God's perfect will, and yet His humanity fought against God's will. His inner turmoil was so great that His sweat became blood.

His example to us was, in His own words, "Nevertheless, thy will be done." The cross is an intersection of wills: our will and His will.

Thank God we will never face the gravity that Jesus did that night, but we should follow His example whenever there is a conflict of wills. We should do so every day, in the small things and the big things. As we follow Him, we experience a continual process of death, burial, and resurrection in our souls.

> The Lord has to break us down at the strongest part of our self-life before He can have His own way of blessing with us. Fullness of joy is found only in the emptying of the will (Ann Voskamp).

Nothing can bring more happiness than the emptying of our self-will and being filled with His will.

Then He said to them all, If any desires to come after Me, let him deny himself, and take up his cross daily, and follow Me (Luke 9:23).

For if we live, we live to the Lord; and if we die, we die to the Lord, therefore, whether we live or die, we are the Lord's (Romans 14:8).

I affirm, by the boasting in You which I have in Christ Jesus our Lord, I die daily (1 Corinthians 15:31).

I had lived my life with self at the center. I loved Christ with an outward obedience, but my will and desires were always in charge. I was the one calling the shots in my heart of hearts.

When self rules our life, everything is filtered through our own desires, our plan, and our assessment of the situation. We fool ourselves by thinking that if things go our way, we will be happy, and everything will run smoothly. And if things don't go our way, all will be lost. Our foolish thinking tells us that we know what is best for us and that we can do whatever needs to be done. There is something about having power and control that entices us and keeps us from experiencing the freedom that Christ can provide.

The irony of it is that we've seen many times over how trying to figure things out and manipulating people and circumstances has backfired and left a mess to clean up or, even worse, has done irreparable damage. But we still remained unwilling to abandon self and allow Christ His rightful place as the center of all things in life.

It all boils down to trust. If I give up control, can I trust Him to know and do what is best for me? Can I trust that His plan is to be good to me? Will He hurt me or insist on my doing something that I don't want to do, go somewhere I don't want to go, or, even worse, change who I am? Simple thinking keeps us from coming into all we are created to be and fulfilling the wonderful plan for our life.

We mistakenly think of death as being final, but death with Christ is always followed by resurrection and new life. If Christ asks us to die to something—to give something up—it is always so that He can replace it with something of eternal value. He is always motivated by love and the desire to give us something back.

I had lived my life thinking that if I ever fully gave Him my life, He would be in control, and I would somehow always be taken from. Foolish thinking. God is a lover and a giver, a God of multiplication and not subtraction.

When I finally came to the place of total surrender, it was like the lights came on. I had been living in the dark, and someone flipped the switch. Freedom came into the deepest part of my soul, and I experienced unexplainable release. I was released from being responsible for myself, and now I would rest in the loving arms of my Lord and Savior Jesus Christ.

He is always good, and we are always loved.

Greater love has no one than this than to lay down one's life for his friends (John 15:13).

When we understand His love for us, we can trust Him.

Chapter 9

Can I Trust Him?

Trust in the Lord with all your heart; do not depend on your own understanding. Seek His will in all you do and He will show you what path to take (Proverbs 3:5–6 NLT)

And I am convinced that nothing can ever separate us from God's love. Neither death nor life, neither angels or demons, neither our fears for today nor our worries about tomorrow—not even the powers of hell can separate us from God's love. No power in the sky above or in the earth below—indeed, nothing in all creation will ever be able to separate us from the love of God that is revealed in Christ Jesus our Lord (Romans 8:38–39 NLT).

It is easier to obey God than to trust God.

God is completely sovereign.

God is infinite in wisdom.

God is perfect in love.

Some have said, "God in His love always wills what is best of us. In His wisdom He always knows what is best, and in His sovereignty He has the power to bring it about."

Who can speak and have it happen if the Lord has not decreed it? Is it not from the mouth of the Most High that both calamities and good things come? (Lamentations 3:37–38).

Since God is in control of (sovereign) in both good and calamity, we should be comforted by it. Whatever the calamity or adversity, we can be sure that God has a loving purpose in it. King Hezekiah said, "Surely it was for my benefit that I suffered anguish" (Isaiah 38:17).

The Lord brings the counsel of the nations to nothing; He makes the plans of the peoples of no effect. The counsel of the Lord stands forever, The plans of His heart to all generations (Psalm 33:10–11).

Consider the work of God; for who can make straight what He has made crooked? (Ecclesiastes 7:13).

There are many plans in a man's heart, nevertheless the Lord's counsel—that will stand (Proverbs 19:21).

Jerry Bridges, in his book *Trusting God,* states, "God has a purpose and a plan for you, and God has the power to carry out that plan! It is one thing to know that no person or circumstance can touch us outside of God's sovereign control; it is still another to realize that no person or circumstance can frustrate God's purpose for our lives.

God has an overarching purpose for all believers: to conform us to the likeness of His Son, Jesus Christ (Romans 8:29). He also has a specific purpose for each of us, that is, His unique, tailor-made plan for our individual lives (Ephesians 2:10). And God will fulfill that purpose. As Psalm 138:8(Message) says, "The Lord will fulfill His purpose for me. Because we know God is directing our lives to an ultimate end and because we know He is sovereignly able to orchestrate the events of our lives toward that end, we can trust Him. We can commit to Him not only the ultimate outcome of our lives, but also all the intermediate events and circumstances that will bring us to that outcome."

Ruth was an example of how God sovereignly worked out His wonderful plan and blessed her through what could have been considered tragedy in her life and family.

Joseph did not have an easy rise to his place of destiny, but his trust in God's sovereignty and great love kept him confident of his ultimate outcome.

God is able to take all of the disappointments, tragedies, and injustices in life and make full use of them. He can turn them into building blocks that form our character and bring us great success.

God's wisdom is seen in bringing good out of evil and beauty out of ashes.

Because of His great love for us we can trust Him with the unanswered questions and the unexplainable scenarios of our lives.

You can trust the One who means all things for your good. He will make your desert a spring.

God has made me fruitful in the land of my grief (Genesis 41:52).

The way Joseph handled his adversity paved the way for his blessing in the land of his grief. Our adversity can destroy us or lift us to a higher place; it all depends on our perspective. God's plan is always at work.

We must see all of life from the perspective of God's Word and His character. All new life is formed through difficult and dark places in our lives.

Regardless of what has happened to you in the past, God is good. Regardless of what is going on in your life right now, God is good.

"For I know the plans I have for you," says the Lord. "They are plans for good and not for disaster, to give you a future and a hope" (Jeremiah 29:11).

Your present circumstances will not last forever.

The life of mortals is like grass, they flourish like a flower of the field...but from everlasting to everlasting the Lord's love is with those who fear Him and His righteousness with their children's children (Psalm 103:15, 17).

Then they cried out to the Lord in their

troubles and He delivered them from their distress. He led them by a straight way to a city where they could settle. Let them give thanks to the Lord for His unfailing love (Psalm 107:6–8).

Shout for joy, you heavens; rejoice, you earth; burst into singing, you mountains, for the Lord comforts His people and will have compassion on His afflicted ones (Isaiah 49:13).

I know firsthand that it is difficult to reconcile the goodness of God in the midst of heart-wrenching situations. Mistakes, abuse, human tragedy, and injustice have a way of clouding our vision. Pain and suffering are difficult to see as gifts from God especially when they affect the lives of people we love. Tragedy will eclipse God's love and His goodness, if we allow it to do so.

I love Ann Voskamp's statement: "God is good, and I am always loved." Even when I don't see it or feel it, truth remains truth. In our times of desperation we must anchor our souls in the goodness and sovereignty of God. Without this anchor, the tragedies will destroy us. But the anchor of God's goodness in all things will bring us through, not with sadness, but with victory.

There are far too many tragedies in life and too few testimonies of God's goodness through it all. Finding God in the middle of our situation will completely turn it around for good. We will ultimately view the situation as a gift and not a curse or punishment. God is always there; we simply must find Him.

I began the journey of tragedy as just another statistic—just another mishap of nature, just another family headed for the rocks. But along the way we got it. We said no to the "reliability" of statistics and yes to God's sovereignty. We said no to the defeat that was projected on our little family and yes to a journey with a purpose, with a God who had a plan and an end.

> *You have heard of the perseverance of Job and seen the end intended by the Lord—that the Lord is very compassionate and merciful (James 5:11).*

God is good.

God brings conclusions to situations. He brings value and worth from our suffering and somehow, as only as He can, "makes all things beautiful in their season."

When I first started my journey, no one could have convinced me that anything beautiful could ever come out of it. I saw only destruction and devastation. Sometimes we just have to find something to hold onto and keep walking toward the other side.

Somewhere in the middle of it all we came face to face with the God of the Bible. Sometimes He reveals Himself as the God of the burning bush or the God who parted the Red Sea. Sometimes He reveals Himself in something as small and insignificant as a coffee cup on which is printed the words "You Can Make It!" When God comes, know that you can trust Him.

Chapter 10

Forgiveness Isn't an Option

Watch out that no poisonous root of bitterness grows up to trouble you, corrupting many (Hebrews 12:15 NLT).

Forgiveness is never about the offender, but is all about those who do the forgiving. Hated and revenge lock us in a cell from which there is no escape, but forgiveness liberates us to be free from the offense and the offender.

Not even the smallest root of unforgiveness can remain. The tiniest of seeds left will eventually sprout and grow into bitterness that produces death and destruction.

Dear one, may I speak directly to you? Whatever your

circumstances, I know your pain. I have been there; I know injustice, abuse, isolation, and heartache. Let it all go. Forgive, and release the offense and the offender. If there is vengeance to be paid, God is much better at it than we are. He has the power to make the penalty equal to the offense.

> *O Lord God to whom vengeance belongs (Psalm 94:1).*

> *Beloved do not avenge yourselves, but rather give place to wrath; for it is written, "Vengeance is Mine, I will repay," says the Lord (Romans 12:19).*

When we choose to forgive and allow God to be the judge, He will not only see that justice is served on wrongdoers, but He will also reward those who were offended.

> *And when you stand praying, if you have anything against anyone, forgive him that your Father in heaven may also forgive you your trespasses. But if you do not forgive, neither will your Father in heaven forgive your trespasses (Mark 11:25–26).*

Forgiveness is the first step out of our bondage.

Remember that Job was healed when he forgave (prayed for) his friends, who had wrongly accused him.

And the Lord restored Job's losses when he prayed for his friends (Job 42:10).

Indeed the Lord gave Job twice as much as he had before.

Had I held onto the pain and injustices that Rebekah was subjected to, I'm sure I would not be the whole person that I am today. I am quite sure that I would have had a complete mental and emotional breakdown, and my body would be eaten alive with the disease that unforgiveness produces.

Forgiveness is not an emotion or a process of forgetting, and it does not mean making light of the offense. Forgiveness is a choice. Jesus prayed for Father God to forgive His enemies while He was suspended on Calvary's cross. Physically tortured, spiritually tormented, and mentally tried, the Lord made a choice to forgive. His request was obviously an act of His will, and not just an emotion. Likewise, Stephen asked God to forgive his accusers as he was being stoned.

The first consequence of unforgiveness is spiritual death. When we don't forgive others, God doesn't forgive us.

Another destructive consequence of unforgiveness is emotional depression. Mental side effects flow from depression.

And then there are the physical consequences of not forgiving. The human body cannot function properly with a spiritual cancer eating away at it. Anger, bitterness, and hatred have an adverse effect on the body. Many illnesses, such as heart disease, high blood pressure, and ulcers, follow.

We cannot afford to continue carrying hatred and unforgiveness. I believe this is why the Lord made sure that I had forgiven each and every person that had caused us pain. Forgiveness freed me so I could receive healing and move forward with my life.

Many of the people whom I forgave had no idea that they had wronged us, and no clue that I was holding animosity in my heart toward them. They were going on with their lives, probably not even remembering us. But I knew, and it was eating me alive.

I am so glad that the Lord made me face my pain, instructed me to release the offenders, and let the pain go. It was not easy—it never is—but it set me free. I don't have to live with revenge seething just under the surface that can, at any moment and with the right trigger, consume my being with the bile of an unforgiving heart.

Let it go, so you can be free and live free.

Chapter 11

The Unfolding Plan

Surely, just as I have intended so it has happened and just as I have planned so it will stand (Isaiah 14:24 NASB [New American Standard Bible]).

The everlasting arms of God had led me, chastened me, directed me, carried me, and now enabled me to comprehend His love and mercy as He revealed His plan for my precious Rebekah.

When our journey began our goal was life at any cost. Every thought and action focused on the fight for Rebekah's life. In the hospital, in meetings with the doctors, and at home, everything was all about the fight for Rebekah to live. And she did. We reached the point where she was almost three years old, a toddler in the normal world. Her body was growing and so was her reality of her own bondage. It became harder and harder for her to deal with her blindness and physical limitations.

As I gazed into her beautiful face and big blue eyes, I became aware of what real love is. Real love goes beyond what we want and begins to consider the big picture for the ones we love. My prayer had always been, "Lord, heal her. " Now I saw a little girl struggling to deal with a body that wouldn't respond in a world so small that all of the earth's beauty was lost to her forever. More than I wanted her to be healed, I wanted her to be free.

I began to pray, "Lord, heal Rebekah or take her home." I wanted her to be free from her bondage—no matter how. I think that when I began to pray just for her to be free, real love kicked in. We had prayed every prayer that we knew to pray. We had her on every prayer chain that we could contact.

Mom and Dad's church was in revival and a minister that we knew was conducting the meeting. He was a man of great faith and believed in miracles. I had my Dad check with him to see if I could have a private meeting with him, and he graciously set a time.

The trip that morning took about an hour, and on the way, I rehearsed the details of my story. I was fully convinced in my heart that after he heard my story, he would say, "Sister, let's grab hold of the horns of the altar and believe God and pray this miracle through."

The minister and I were escorted to the pastor's small office where we encountered that same presence of God that had met me at Christian Retreat. There are no words that can express the love that filled the little room. The minister who had provided so much truth and encouragement for so many years listened to me with great compassion. I told the story, trying not to leave anything out. I wanted him to know all that had happened. I shared with him how I prayed for the Lord to heal Rebekah or take her home.

I will always remember his words as he began to share what I would realize later was God's voice to me. He said, "Sister, sometimes we hold on too long." As he talked to me, it felt like two large arms came up under me and enabled me to bear what was being said. What great grace.

With great love and compassion the minister shared with me that as a young minister just starting out in the faith ministry, he had a friend that had four daughters. One of those daughters became sick with a terminal disease. He listened as his friend prayed, "Lord, I love my daughter, she is a gift from You. I ask You to heal her. If You choose to touch her and raise her up and give her back to me, I will praise You. If You choose to take her home to heal her, I will praise You as her spirit goes to be with You."

The minister shared with me how he struggled with his friend's concept of healing. He said that he came to understand that going home is not second best. It is not a consolation prize; it is home. He saw that there are some things that only God knows, and that we have to trust His justice and love.

So he said, "Brenda, we will pray and God will heal Rebekah. He will either touch her, raise her up, and give her back to you, or He will take her home." We prayed, releasing Rebekah to the God that sent her to us, and we entrusted her to His sovereign plan for her good.

When we were finished praying and were making preparations to leave, the minister turned to me and said, "If God chooses to take her home, you'll just go in to get her one morning and she will be gone. She will never have to be handed over to doctors again. No more needles, no more mistakes, no more pain."

The minister never said to me that God was going to take our precious Rebekah home to heal her, but the voice of God did. I heard it loud and clear; there was no doubt, no misunderstanding. I knew in the deepest part of my soul that God was telling me that He would take her home. Those were not the words that I had expected to hear; this was not the outcome that I had anticipated. How do you process this kind of information? My child is going to die, but she will be healed. I know that I would not have been able to bear this understanding without the undergirding of those big arms that had enveloped me when we went into the pastor's office.

On the drive home my mind went into a thousand directions. I was elated knowing that my Becky would be free, but how could I rejoice when knowing that her freedom meant physical death? How can you rejoice in death? How can you celebrate death? How would I tell Frank? How would I tell my parents who had fought so long and hard for life and battled the enemy, and believed for a miracle. I cried with grief and rejoiced for victory in the same moment.

When I got home I shared with Frank my experience and what God had said to me through the minister. The truth was so real, there was no denying that I had heard the voice of God. The same grace that enabled me to bear the understanding was there for Frank. It was much more difficult for my parents. They had been so faithful in their fight for Rebekah's life. It was OK. We each had to process the truth in our own way. Frank would later say to me, "How do I praise God for healing my daughter, when I know that that means her death? How do I thank God for healing her, knowing that we will lose her?"

For the next thirteen months we praised and thanked God for Rebekah's healing, and we chose to let God do it His way, which ultimately was best. We chose to allow God do the things that He alone can know. We trusted in His justice, His love, and His plan to always do what is good and right. We came to realize that there are a lot of things worse than death.

God was gracious in that He allowed two wonderful women of God to confirm what He had told me about His plan to take Rebekah home. I never told anyone outside our little family. The Lord told these two ladies and when I inquired of them if they had heard anything, they shared that God had revealed to them His plan. I am so glad I had these confirmations so there wouldn't be any chance to doubt or misunderstand God's plan.

Chapter 12

Time to Settle the Issues

He is the Rock, His deeds are perfect. Everything He does is just and fair. He is a faithful God who does no wrong; how just and upright He is! (Deuteronomy 32:4 NLT).

As we waited for Rebekah's healing, God was doing great work in our hearts. There were so many issues that had to be addressed. We all had our own struggles with the knowledge that Becky's freedom meant that she would leave us. We didn't know when, but we knew that God's plan would mean victory for her.

One of the first issues that I was made aware of was forgiveness. Rebekah had suffered so much at the hands of doctors who made gigantic mistakes, nurses who had to be stopped from overdosing medications, and lab technicians who caused her horrendous pain. It seemed like she had lived in a torture chamber for those seven months in the hospital. She couldn't comprehend that everything that was done was meant for her good. She only knew the pain she experienced.

I had done much work on forgiveness earlier. But God said that "not even the smallest root of unforgiveness could remain." The tiniest acorn left in the ground undisturbed will eventually grow into a mighty oak.

As I sat in the rocking chair, loving on my sweet Rebekah, God would cause me to remember something or someone who had made a mistake or caused pain. I would choose to forgive them and release them. The more I forgave, the freer I became. The terrible images or memories of encounters would never again be an issue.

This small, fragile girl was teaching me so much about our Creator. How could she know so much? How could she know Him so well?

As I would sit with her and look into those eyes, the mother part of me would struggle. I knew that she would be leaving me, I knew that it was best for her, but how could I let her go? In one of those moments, God said something to me that set me free. He said, "Brenda, as soon as she gets here, I will tell her everything. I will tell her how much you love her, I will tell her why she came, why she suffered, and I will make it all right with her. " God would bring justice to Rebekah. I could envision her listening to Father God, hearing Him tell her what He had used her to do in my life, and then seeing her smile and say, "OK. If my suffering accomplished so much in my Mother's life, then it was worth it."

Because Rebekah came to the earth in the purposes of God, to be used by Him to accomplish His will, and to give her life to His will, she will receive a martyr's crown. And on judgment day when the crowns are given out, she will stand head and shoulders with all the martyrs who gave their life for Christ. And every life that is touched through Frank and me will go to her credit.

As the journey continued, God reminded me of the long and agonizing nights when there was so much darkness and pain, and of how I cried out and begged for help, and there was none. He told me that He held me in the palm of His hand. He showed me that He was always in charge of the amount of pressure in my life. He had to allow the pressure. It was designed to break me, but He would have never allowed it to crush me. It was that pressure that brought me to the end of myself, where I could finally be free. We can trust a loving God who is always in charge of the stresses in life. He will not allow them to destroy us, but will use them to free us.

As the months passed we were put in contact with a church in North Florida that gave us an opportunity to return to full-time ministry. The decision to move six hours away from my parents was a very weighty choice to make. Moving there would mean that I wouldn't have any help with Rebekah. Although her pain was gone, she still required constant attention. Because of her blindness she only felt secure and safe in our arms, so she spent most of her waking hours in our laps in the rocking chair. We fed her goat's milk with a syringe, and she could eat baby cereal and pureed baby foods. Sometimes she could nap in her swing, but for the most part we held her.

If we moved so far away, I would have it all to do myself. There would be meals, laundry, Miranda's care, and my husband. And yes, I would also be the pastor's wife.

We prayed a lot, sought counsel, and came to the conclusion that it was God's will for us to go. Mom and Dad took Rebekah to their house while we packed and moved, and came up later to get her settled in. All I had ever wanted was to take care of my little family on my own as any mother would. I wanted to be a good wife, to be a mother to Miranda and Rebekah, and to take care of my home. I had the chance now, but how could it be done? God's grace was the way.

When Mom and Dad went home, we worked out a system. It was very hard, but we worked together. So there we were—the four of us, as we had started out.

The people at the church were kind and loving; they felt touched when they came into contact with Rebekah. She had the glow of God's presence on her, and it affected everyone who got close to her. You somehow knew that she was part of God's purpose on the earth.

For thirteen months, God settled every issue, answered every question, and revealed to us what it would mean for

Rebekah to go home. Heaven had become a real place, not a separation from but an extension of this life. He showed us that the day she would go home would be her coronation day, a day of celebration. Our loss would truly be heaven's gain.

The struggle to embrace death as a good thing had been replaced with the reality of Rebekah's freedom, justice for her suffering, and the reality that the next time we see her we would walk and talk with her for as long as we wanted.

God was gracious to give us that time to know His plan, process our thoughts, and come to an eternal perspective. Mom and Dad continued to have faith in God's best. Faithfully, they helped us, prayed, fought the enemy, and poured their lives into our family. We couldn't have made it without them.

We fought many battles. The enemy would attack Rebekah with sickness and pain. On more than one occasion, she would stop eating, which was serious because the G-tube had been removed. If she did not take in liquids within a certain time frame, we would have to have to tube reinstalled, and that was never an option.

Mom and Dad would also call the prayer chain at their church, where Rebekah had prayer support on a daily basis. A little while after the intercessors would begin to pray, Rebekah would begin to smack. That was Daddy's signal to get the bottle. Time and time again, we went to battle, and every time God gave us the victory.

On one occasion Rebekah became sick, and the doctor

ordered X-rays. He said that if the X-rays showed pneumonia, she would have to be hospitalized. We continued to stand firm on the word that the man of God had said, that we would never again have to hand her over to the hospital. While waiting for the results, my mom, who was holding Rebekah, gave her to me and said, "I have to go somewhere and talk out loud to the devil." Sometimes that is what a situation calls for: we have to raise our voices to our enemies, who would like to steal from our families. Well, Momma did talk out loud to the devil, and the technician came out soon afterward and told us that there were no signs of pneumonia. We took Becky home and cared for her, and she recovered quickly. At a follow-up appointment with the pediatrician he looked at the X-rays, pointed to a white spot, and said, "This is pneumonia." Yes it was, but God took care of it His way.

During the time of our greatest intensity of struggle, there was a heaviness in the atmosphere of our home. You could feel the resistance against your chest as you walked from one end of the house to the other. There was no joy, no peace, and certainly no victory.

In the midst of this, God instructed Frank that, before he got out of bed in the morning, he was to lift his hands and worship. Frank said that at first his arms were like lead; he could only hold them up for very short periods of time, but he wouldn't give up. He continued to do as the Lord instructed. It wasn't long before the heaviness began to lift, and God used this to bring us out.

As part of our unity as a family, Frank called Miranda and me together and told us that we were a family and families stick together, so we were going to have a family motto. Our motto is this: "We're not going to let this lick us; we're going to let it lift us." We may not always have control over our circumstances, but we always have control of what we allow them to do to us. Our attitude will determine if we come out on the other side as victims or victors. We chose to be victors. We had a situation that could bury all of us, but we knew that God promised to use the things that were intended to destroy us to make us better. We chose better! When things would get difficult, one of us would call out, "Family Motto!" We would get into our little circle of three and proclaim with great confidence, "We're not going to let this lick us; we're going to let it lift us."

One summer when things had settled down somewhat, Mom and Dad kept Rebekah for a week so that we could take a vacation. We went to PTL (known as the PTL Club with the Bakkers in South Carolina) we had wonderful vacations there in the past. While there, we tried to enter into normal activities for families, but our hearts were broken, and having fun even for Miranda's sake was very difficult. We were constantly searching for even a ray of hope for our future. While in the gift shop, we found white coffee mugs with large red letters that said, "You can make it!" We bought a dozen mugs. When we would have our coffee in the morning, the message brought us hope. Yes, we are going to make it ! Along with the mugs on that vacation, the Lord gave us a scripture to hold onto:

> *You've seen the end of the Lord in Job's life,*
> *and God is good (James 5:11).*

We clung to the coffee cups, but, what is more, the Word put hope in our hearts.

A Special Presence

God's justice has never been more demonstrated in my life than during my three-and-a-half-year journey with Rebekah. Sometimes people can alter the truth with their own scales. They place weights on the scales in order to have the advantage over others. They try to shift things toward themselves, making things one-sided. It is not so with God. His weights are just and sure.

Rebekah came to us to fulfill God's purpose in our lives, and as such she paid a big price. God is just and righteous, so He had to compensate her along the way. He would come to her and supply, to her degree of suffering, grace for her journey. We are aware of three occasions that Jesus visited Rebekah. On one occasion, she was at Mom's house. Mother had her in her lap and was singing and worshiping the Lord. Mother sensed the presence of the Holy Spirit growing stronger and stronger in the room. The room took on an amber glow, and Rebekah began to respond to the presence. Mother said that her eyes became very large, as if she recognized what she saw, and her body began to lift from Mother's lap. Mom could not tell what Rebekah was experiencing, but it was obvious that she had encountered the Lord Jesus.

Throughout her short life, He would come and reveal Himself to her because of her purpose in His plan.

God's justice was also manifested by a special presence that came to our family during the last part of her life.

To the degree of intensity of the load that we carried, God gave us a special awareness of His presence. It was a presence that we had not had in previous times. For the last year and a half, He talked to us continually, He gave special grace in trying times, and we just always knew that He was there and undergirding. It was that grace that sustained us and enabled us to do what we could not do on our own. That grace caused us to survive. And it was grace that brought all to a conclusion and made everything all right.

Possessing My Vessel

During one of my difficult times when internal pressure was increasing and about to explode, as if in a pressure cooker, I was doing everything in my power to keep from ripping my clothes off and running, screaming, through the streets. I knew that the pressure was real, and I knew God's grace was mine, but it seemed as if the pressure would win this time. What do you do? You reach out and let grace come. Frank asked me, "What are you doing?" I told him, "I'm possessing my vessel." That's the only way I could explain it—I was trying to maintain the truth of God's Word as my fortress, so that the things inside it would not take over and destroy me.

When the pressures of life seem like they will overtake you, and you want to take the top off of the pressure cooker and let everything explode into the atmosphere, don't. There is a better way. The military terms it "staying the course. " In that moment when we choose to be in charge of our vessel (our body, our mind, and our emotions) and we choose not to allow the pressure to win, God's grace will come. He will turn down the fire under the pressure cooker.

There were many times that I had to reply completely upon God's grace as I possessed my vessel.

Chapter 13

Heaven's Gain

We are confident, yes, well pleased rather to be absent from the body and to be present with the Lord (2 Corinthians 5:8).

During the last year of Rebekah's life, it seemed like we were just supposed to hold her, love her, kiss her, and enjoy this precious life. We were not to focus on how much energy her care required, but simply to love her. We had already stopped all efforts at therapy to advance her physical progress. We didn't want to push her anymore or further her pain or discomfort.

We went through bouts of respiratory infections, even pneumonia, but, as the minister had said to me, we would never have to hand her over to doctors or hospitals again.

We had been at the church in North Florida for six months and had been making it. Mom and Dad would come every couple of months and give us a reprieve. God was so faithful to allow me to take care of my little family. Months before I had awakened in the night and knew that the Holy Spirit wanted to say something to me. I went to the living room and began to pray. The Lord showed me that Rebekah's chariot was on the hillside and was waiting for the command to come for her. I knew by this sign that it would not be long.

The day was February 24, 1989. I remember that day Rebekah had not wanted to eat. It had been a struggle to get food and drink into her. I was exhausted, but all I could do was kiss her all day. I had no clue what was happening. I kissed every part of her beautiful face. Even now I can see in my mind's eye the curve of her nose and feel my lips as they kissed it. I didn't think that it was a good thing to kiss babies in the mouth, but that day I did. I kissed her lips, I kissed her nose, I kissed her eyes, I kissed her chin, and I kissed her forehead and her cheeks and ears. I kissed her little hand and fingers. I can remember pressing her little hand to my lips and drinking in the beauty and value of her life. She had given me so much; she had brought me so far. God had used her to transform my life.

Tired and exhausted from the day, I put her to bed for the night. I finished putting Miranda to bed and collapsed into bed myself.

On February 25, 1989, at 5:45 a.m., I went in to Rebekah's room and found, just as the man of God had said, that "she was gone."

That same presence that had accompanied God's voice to me in the past was with me there. The same everlasting arms were there for me now. As I looked at the tiny shell that had held Rebekah captive, my heart overflowed with gratitude that she was finally free. She was safe and secure in her heavenly Father's arms. She now knew everything, and He had made all things all right with her.

Remorse hit me because I had not been there with her as she crossed from this life to the next, but God assured me that she was not alone and that she was never in darkness. We can only go so far with our children. In that moment she did not need my hand, but the hand of the one who had been faithful to her for her short three and a half years of life.

Nothing could have prepared me for holding in my arms the little body where she had lived. Her spirit was gone, her shell empty. How would we ever live without her presence and the presence of God that surrounded her?

We made the necessary calls, and before long the house was filled with officials. After they finished, the gentleman from the funeral home came to take her body. Later he told us that he usually drove a van to pick up a body, but on this day, Rebekah's day, he drove a big white Cadillac.

I brushed her hair, kissed her one more time, wrapped her in her blanket, and put her into his arms.

Frank and I went to the window to watch. The sun was

just coming up and the dew sparkled in the sunshine. The car was parked in what looked like a big courtyard. The gentleman placed Rebekah gently in the backseat and started the car. Everything seemed to go into slow motion.

He pulled the car around in a large circle, and as the sun shone on the car, it glistened like something heavenly. As he made his wide sweep around the courtyard, it looked as though the car would lift up and go straight into heaven.

As he drove away with our precious baby girl, we were left standing at the window. We immediately realized that the special grace and awareness of God's presence, which had enabled us to live in such a situation, had lifted. She was gone, and we no longer needed that special grace. It was such a loss that we agreed that we would walk through it all over again to get that presence back.

We spent time with Miranda, explaining what had happened, and we called Mom and Dad who were visiting but had traveled a short distance to visit my grandmother. By the time we came out of Miranda's room, our house was full of church people. There was a large pot of coffee brewing and trays of biscuits and sausage. A woman had even put up the ironing board and was ironing our clothes. They poured out their love on our little family.

Mom and Dad returned to our home, and we made preparations to place our sweet girl in Winter Haven, Florida, where Mom and Dad lived, so they could watch over her gravesite.

We had her service at Mom and Dad's church, which had been so faithful to pray for us all. The minister who conducted Rebekah's service clearly understood her purpose, and we made her funeral service a celebration of her life and God's goodness.

In his message, he communicated that this small child was sent to the earth not to ride a bicycle, play with a baby doll, or take part in any childhood game. Instead, she was sent as part of God's plan to captivate the hearts of her parents and lead them to a greater understanding of Him and His ways. He said that God straightens every crooked path, brings the low place high, and brings justice in all of life.

There is always a far greater purpose at work than we can see in our momentary suffering. If we have patience enough to wait, we will see the fulfillment of God's goodness.

On Rebekah's gravestone we have written, "From Your Heart to Ours She Came, From Our Heart to Yours She Returned." God truly carved out part of His heart and placed it in the body of a tiny girl born with Down syndrome, a girl who suffered at the hands of others but all the while led them to better know the One who sent her. "And a little child shall lead them." Praise God for His goodness that loves us too much to leave us the way we are.

I never heard her speak a word, and I never heard her call me Mama, but she was God's voice to me.

Thank you, my darling Rebekah.

Conclusion

There were three other adults that traveled this journey with me, and I am sure that each of them could tell a story of the love of God demonstrated in their lives, because they, too, were touched by Rebekah's life. I will be forever grateful for my parents and the role they had in this season. They were gladly willing to give up their lives in order to help us. But, after all, as I heard someone say recently, that's what families do.

As the minister stood over Rebekah's three-foot-long casket, he spoke to the people gathered to celebrate her life. He said that she was no twist of fate, no mistake, but a love gift from God sent to guide her parents. She was, in her parents' words, "God's voice" to them. And when her task was complete, God took her to Himself to adequately reward her for a job well done.

He talked about how, in heaven, God makes everything all right. He takes all of the injustices of life and brings justice. He makes the crooked places straight, and He brings the high places low and the low places high. And in that place Rebekah is forever free to enjoy the light that radiates from Christ.

We never know what we will be called upon to walk through in this life, but one thing is sure: "God is good, and He does good, and we are always loved, and above the clouds, the light is always shining." If we will allow Him, He will bring beauty from our ashes and turn our sorrow into joy. Like David, He will put steel in our veins and use the most insignificant people to accomplish great work for

His glory.

Please don't waste your tears; give them to Jesus, and let Him transform you.

A. W. Tozer said, "God can't use a man or a woman until they have been hurt deeply." How can we comfort others until we have been comforted?

Corrie ten Boom said, "In order to realize the worth of the anchor we need to feel the stress of the storm."

Frank and I continue to walk through each door that presents itself, and we have found Him who called us to be faithful to walk with us. We are forever changed by Rebekah's life. We look forward to the day that we will speak to her face to face, take her by the hand, and "stroll over heaven together."

The rose that lives its little hour

Is prized beyond the sculptured flower

(William Cullen Bryant,
A Scene on the Banks of the Hudson).

Why things happen as they do

we do not always know,

And we cannot always fathom

why our spirits sink so low

…

For though we are incapable,

God's powerful and great

And there's no darkness or distress

That God cannot penetrate

…

And all that is required of us

whenever things go wrong

Is to trust in God implicitly with

a faith that's deep and strong

…

And in His time, if we have faith,

He will gradually restore

The brightness to our spirits that

we've been longing for

…

So remember, there's no cloud too

dark for God's light to penetrate

If we keep on believing and

have faith enough to wait.

(Helen Steiner Rice, *Love Gifts*).

Author's Page

Brenda Adams is a seasoned minister and experienced author with her articles appearing in national publications. Brenda currently serves with her husband as co-pastor of their church in Triangle, Va.

Brenda has a daughter Miranda who lives in the Washington, D.C. area with her husband Todd and their son Bennett.

Brenda is a dynamic public speaker who speaks with boldness, clarity and relevance to the subjects she addresses. Audiences discover that her humor and life experiences combine to give great insight, help and hope to those who hear her message.

For more information, or if you would like to have Brenda speak at your event or church, please contact her at:

Soldout2him

www.soldout2him.com

booking@soldout2him.com

See Rebekah's photo album on the website